T3-BPE-240

FINANCIAL SECTOR OF THE AMERICAN ECONOMY

edited by
STUART BRUCHEY
ALLAN NEVINS PROFESSOR EMERITUS
COLUMBIA UNIVERSITY

A GARLAND SERIES

FIRM VALUE
AND OPTIMAL LEVELS
OF LIQUIDITY

J. EDWARD GRAHAM

GARLAND PUBLISHING, INC.
A MEMBER OF THE TAYLOR & FRANCIS GROUP
NEW YORK & LONDON / 2001

658.152
G73f

Published in 2001 by
Garland Publishing, Inc.
29 West 35th Street
New York, NY 10001

Garland Publishing is an imprint of the Taylor & Francis Group

ⁿ Copyright © 2000 by J. Edward Graham

All rights reserved. No part of this book may be reprinted or reproduced or utilized in any form or by any electronic, mechanical, or other means, now known or hereafter invented, including photocopying and recording, or in any information storage or retrieval system, without written permission from the publishers.

10 9 8 7 6 5 4 3 2 1

Library of Congress Cataloguing-in-Publication Data available through Library of Congress

ISBN 0-8153-3802-3 (alk. paper)

Printed on acid-free, 250 year-life paper
Manufactured in the United States of America

Dedication and Acknowledgements

This book is dedicated to my wife, my mother and my father.

Credit is due every person in my life for the patience, understanding and encouragement shown me over the past five or six years. The following gentleman, however, deserve an extra tip of the hat for the lengths to which each of them has gone on my behalf. No gesture by me could ever begin adequately to describe my gratitude for the time and energy each has given me. Since entering college:

Dr. Joe Goldsten, at Washington and Lee University,
Dr. Stephen Shapiro, at the University of North Florida,
Dr. Tim Koch, at the University of South Carolina,
Dr. Kin Blackburn, at the University of South Carolina,
Dr. Greg Niehaus, for his compassion, at the University of South Carolina, and
Dr. LeRoy Brooks, also at the University of South Carolina, my chairman, my confidant and my mentor; for having a sense of humor when nothing seemed at all funny, to him I owe the greatest professional acknowledgement.

University Libraries
Carnegie Mellon University
Pittsburgh, PA 15213-3890

Preface

The objective here is to consider the factors influencing a firm's optimal level of liquidity. Financial theory describes the demand for liquid resources by the firm and the impact of the accumulation of liquidity on firm value. Studies by Miller and Orr (1966,1968), Myers and Majluf (1984), Jensen (1986) and Stulz (1990) establish that firm value is first enhanced and later reduced as the firm acquires liquid resources. Combining the ideas of Myers and Majluf (1984) and Jensen (1986), the optimal level of liquidity is determined by costs of over- and under-investment and the carrying and stockout costs portrayed by Miller and Orr (1966,1968). Capital markets favor the inflow of needed liquidity to avoid stockout costs, but penalize firm value for liquidity's carrying costs. Investors' reactions to liquidity changes and knowledge of the variables related to these costs should provide evidence of the optimal liquidity position.

Private equity placement announcements are examined as they provide an opportunity to study changes in firm value, at the time of an announced change in liquidity, independent of issues that may obscure the sources of changes in firm value in other liquidity-enhancing events. Prior studies of private placements provide little or no evidence on the impact of liquidity enhancement on firm value. This study considers the premise that market responses to these announcements are conditioned, in part, by a firm's access to liquid resources. Since prior studies attribute market responses to these announcements to information releases and changes in ownership structure, controls are provided for these and other firm-specific features. A sample of private placement announcements between 1988 and 1995 is examined. Abnormal returns are adjusted for the size and price of the placement. Significant unadjusted and adjusted positive abnormal returns are discovered over the primary announcement period. This contrasts with adverse market responses to equity issues in general, but is consistent with the positive responses to private placements observed in prior studies.

Selected liquidity measures are significantly related to market responses to private placement announcements. Given the substantial costs borne by the firm in placing equity privately, a pecking order model of capital structure is favored over a static tradeoff model. Pre-announcement liquidity and changes in liquidity are, independently and interactively, positively and significantly related to these market responses. Changes in liquidity are significantly more important than a firm's initial liquidity levels in describing market reactions to these announcements. Most proxies for managerial discretion are not significantly related to the market's responses, but changes in ownership concentration pursuant to the private placement are associated with non-monotonic changes in firm value. An earnings/price ratio and firm size are significantly and inversely related to observed abnormal returns. The earnings/price and firm size measures are robust factors in a number of estimating environments. Additionally, recent and more relaxed SEC guidelines reduce the significance of the positive impact, observed in earlier private placement studies, of an unregistered private equity sale.

Moderate existing liquidity prior to the announcement is positively related to market responses, when the size of the liquidity change is ignored. When the size of the liquidity enhancement is considered, however, it dominates. Recent stock performance, similar to existing liquidity levels, may proxy for the announcing firm's survivability, as a significant and adverse market response is observed for the firm underperforming the market in the weeks prior to the announcement.

Table of Contents

List of Tables

List of Figures

CHAPTER 1

Firm Value and Optimal Levels of Liquidity

1.1 Introduction and Motivation

Studies by Miller and Orr (1966, 1968), Myers and Majluf (1984), Jensen (1986) and Stulz (1990) theoretically establish the condition that firm value (stock price) is first increased and later reduced as the firm acquires costly liquid resources. The primary objective of this study is to test the unconfirmed empirical implication of these earlier studies that an optimal level of liquidity exists for the firm. The goal is to measure the strength of the unexamined premise that market responses to private placement announcements are conditioned, in part, by a firm's access to, and need for, financial slack or liquid resources.

The equity-issue puzzle is considered in this study. Implications for a firm's capital structure are specified. Prior examinations of liquidity are extended; the literature on the determinants of stock price responses to private equity issues is supplemented. Much evidence already supports that carrying costs of liquidity and free cash flows can be costly to investors. Little evidence establishes the costliness of stock-outs and under-investment and sacrifice of shareholder value with a slack-poor firm. A growing literature on the costliness of under-investment due to a lack of internal funds is enhanced in the following pages.

Liquidity broadly refers to any firm asset that can be converted to cash or cash equivalents (without a significant price concession) in the current operating cycle relative to the firm's expected cash disbursements over the same period.[1] Liquidity is required to meet operating and growth needs but is often wasted when it is over-accumulated. Liquidity is similar to, but distinct from, financial slack. Financial slack refers to the excess of firm liquidity over the next cycle's (generally one year) needs for operations, debt service and preferred dividends. Capital markets favor the inflow of needed slack, but penalize firm value for the agency costs of free cash flow. An optimal level of liquidity is implied for a given firm based upon its own set of circumstances. The primary contribution of this study comes from determining factors influencing optimal liquidity levels and the consistency of these discoveries with existing theory and prior empirics.

Conceptually, in a perfect market, firm value goes up a dollar with every arriving dollar of liquidity. In an imperfect market, an additional dollar of liquidity may not increase firm value by a dollar. According to Myers and Majluf (1984), putting a dollar of liquidity into the firm creates value as the firm is then relieved of the need to pursue costly external financing. Conversely, Jensen (1986) holds, beyond some point, an arriving dollar of liquidity or financial slack has a negative NPV (Net Present Value) and does not increase existing shareholder wealth by an equal amount. According to Jensen (1986), factors that increase managerial discretion, such as diffuse ownership, lower the optimal liquidity level. Myers and Majluf (1984) suggest that greater investment opportunities and lower degrees of information asymmetries lead to a higher optimal liquidity level. Combining the ideas of Myers and Majluf (1984) and Jensen (1986), the optimal level of liquidity is determined by the costs of over- and under-investment. Their ideas supplement the earlier work of Miller and Orr (1966,1968). They protray carrying and stockout costs arising from excessive and inadequate liquidity investments, respectively. At the optimum, the expected marginal return on the last dollar of slack equals the expected marginal cost of free cash flow for that same dollar.

Ignoring measurement issues and allowing cash and liquid resources to be proxied by selected measures of liquidity and allowing stock price to proxy for firm-value, the valuation effect of additional liquidity is a function of a firm's initial liquidity, the change in liquidity, the firm's liquidity optimum and other factors. This is broadly illustrated by Figure 1 as the firm acquires liquidity and moves to the right along the liquidity axis. Value increases - up to the global minimum cost of liquidity - and then declines.

Developing measures for liquidity and changes in liquidity is fairly straightforward. If multiple controlled observations of liquidity enhancing events for a single firm are made, then a firm-value function - as in Figure 1 - can be developed for that firm. It is much less straightforward for a sample of different firms. Specifying a firm's optimal liquidity level and identifying factors influencing market responses to liquidity enhancing events is difficult. Optimal liquidity is potentially impacted by such issues as ownership structure, growth options, information asymmetries, management compensation and the volatility and correlation among cash inflows and outflows. Equal changes in liquidity imply different changes in firm-value based upon the set of these mitigating factors that impact the costs and benefits of liquidity accumulation.

1.2 Examining an Optimal Liquidity Hypothesis

An optimal liquidity hypothesis holds that market responses to liquidity-changing events are conditioned, in part, by the observed changing levels of firm liquidity. There are many liquidity enhancing events that impact firm-value; debt or equity issues, sales of assets or subdivisions and loans from insiders all provide liquidity. The one choice variable of interest in each of these events is the level of liquidity. The objective of this study is to find a sample of liquidity changes when the sources of the changes in corporate value are as identifiable as possible. A clear link is needed between market responses to corporate events and the liquidity provided as a result of those events.

With a change in liquidity, two points on the functions portrayed in Figures 1-4 can be observed. With this simple infusion, other factors are fixed. But, other factors are not fixed in most liquidity infusions such as when the firm issues securities. News of most liquidity enhancing events is compromised by the resolution of one or more information asymmetries; by its decision to publicly procure funds through the sale of securities or corporate assets, management reveals some degree of inside information.

Separating this information effect from other sources of market responses is difficult. However, the market for private equity placements provides the opportunity to observe market responses to corporate events without the cloud cast by information asymmetries.[2]

Private placements of equity, as noted by Wruck (1989), afford the investigator an opportunity to examine market responses to corporate events without the "clutter" of resolved information asymmetries impacting firm-value. An adjusted abnormal returns measure can be calculated that accounts for much of the resolution of information asymmetries at private placement announcement. Private placements are examined in this study, although the optimal liquidity hypothesis should apply equally to public issues. With the public issues, however, establishing a clear link between changes in shareholder wealth and arriving liquidity is much more tenuous.

1.3 Research Questions

Stock price reaction to liquidity change announcements is a function of initial firm liquidity levels and final levels relative to the firm's optimum. The liquidity optima, in turn, are a function of a number of other factors. For example, a firm with inadequate liquidity, or to the left of the optimum in Figure 1, can expect a favorable market response to a liquidity enhancing event, *ceteris paribus*, achieved by moving towards the optimal level of liquidity. Other relationships between firm value and liquidity levels are portrayed in Figures 2 and 3. Two questions related to these stock price reactions are addressed in this study's consideration of an optimal liquidity hypothesis.

1.3.1 What are the Variables that Affect the Optimal Level of Liquidity and How do these Factors Impact Market Responses to Liquidity Infusions for the Firm?

It is unclear whether available liquidity influences market response to private placement announcements. As Ang (1991) notes, the value of financial slack to the firm and to stockholders is controversial unto itself independent of a firm's financing activities. An examination by Pilotte (1992) finds that slack provides no significant explanatory power to cross-sectional tests of market responses to new external general public offerings. Yet the study by Hertzel and Smith (1993) reveals that firms in financial distress - an indirect proxy for slack poverty - are favorably treated when they announce private placements. Hertzel and Smith (1993) do not, however, examine whether announcement period returns are related to available slack in general. Slack-related variables such as "liquidity," "earnings/price" and "working capital" are adopted in this study and seek to capture that element of the abnormal returns that can potentially be explained by an optimal liquidity hypothesis.

It is important to fill in the existing evidence on the impact of free cash flow with empirics also upon the value of slack. This value can be illustrated at the optimum where the marginal contribution from slack on the next dollar added to liquidity is less than the marginal cost of free cash flow induced by that next dollar. Earlier empirical studies make no specific allowance for the ability of an optimal liquidity hypothesis to explain returns. Examinations by Kim and Smith (1994) and Pilotte (1992) provide contrasting results for the inclusion of a slack factor in cross-sectional studies of market responses to mergers and growing firm security issues, respectively. The former attaches significant value to a slack variable and the latter discourages its inclusion. This contrast provides another catalyst for this study.

1.3.2 *Agency Costs of Free Cash Flow Result When Slack is Accumulated Beyond a Firm's Perceived Needs; Empirically, What are the Implications for Firm-Value for the Privately Placing Firm?*

Funds might be acquired in the public or private market by firms that have sufficient slack; a potential exists for the confounding effects of the agency costs of free cash flow. Capital markets discount firm-value based on levels of this free cash flow vs. the premium provided slack-poor firms as they acquire slack. An extensive literature has grown that documents the market's negative response to the accumulation of liquidity in excess of needs by firms, but no such body has examined the lack of liquidity.[3] The definitions of free cash flow and financial slack are distinct. The proxies used to represent each, however, are similar and their separation is often difficult.

1.4 Private Placements of Equity and the Provision of Liquidity to the Firm

The initial publication of a firms decision to issue equity *privately* is commonly received favorably.[4] This is in contrast with general equity issues that are broadly seen as negative signals by investors.[5] Prior studies (see, for example, Wruck, 1989; Fields and Mais, 1991; and Hertzel and Smith, 1993) attribute these atypical patterns to desirable information releases and improvements in ownership structures as a result of these equity sales. Large and sophisticated individual or institutional investors, by taking a greater investment share of the company, provide a positive opinion about the company's prospects and increase their monitoring of management with the private placement purchase. However, the role of liquidity or financial slack in explaining the average positive returns that occur at announcements of private placements is not considered. Descriptive data in prior research implies that the primary users of private placements may be slack-poor; this condition may increase the likelihood of an observable favorable liquidity effect.

1.5 Limitations of This Study

Several anticipated shortcomings of this study deserve mention.[6] Firms face a number of tradeoffs in selecting private placements and the significance of liquidity in explaining market responses may not be clear; various hypotheses compete for position in explaining empirical test results. The interaction of these hypotheses are only one of the cross-currents that may limit this study. The role played by liquidity in characterizing market responses and in supporting one or another theory of capital and ownership structure are only implied by the relationships between market responses and the explanatory proxies employed.

This dissertation is hampered by data and statistical test limitations and the absence of a "clean" laboratory in which to test differing hypotheses. Published data in the CRSP (Center for Research in Security Prices) and *Compustat* files is often limited for the relatively small and often thinly traded privately issuing firms. The text of the private placement announcements is sometimes inadequate and cursory; these announcements often only partially disclose important placement characteristics. Clear and unequivocal proxies for the underlying hypotheses do not exist. No single telling conclusion is expected. However, these limitations are similar in their spirit to many studies of financial issues and do not preclude a meaningful contribution by this study.

1.6 Empirical Summary

A final sample of 67 private placement announcements are drawn from the *Business News Wire* between 1988 and 1995. Each observation fulfills CRSP, *Compustat* and *Compaq Disclosure* data requirements. Traditional and adjusted market model abnormal returns measures are generated for each firm's announcement over several selected event windows. Ordinary least squares regression analyses are conducted to explain the cross-section of adjusted abnormal returns measures over the primary event window from three days before until the day of the announcement.

Significant adjusted and unadjusted positive abnormal returns are discovered over the primary announcement period. Findings are contrary to expectations of adverse market responses to equity issues in general. Results are similar to favorable responses to private placements observed in prior private placement studies. The infusion of liquidity from the private placements invites market responses that seem to favor a pecking order model over a static tradeoff theory of capital structure. Evidence supports a premise reviewed in this study that ownership structure is less important for the smaller firms in this study than for larger firms in similar studies in describing market responses to news of liquidity enhancing events. Nonetheless, consistent with prior studies on the relationships between firm value and ownership concentration, changes in ownership concentration pursuant to the private placement are associated with non-monotonic changes in firm value. Proxies for growth opportunities and firm size are robust factors in explaining these overall favorable returns. Recent and more relaxed SEC guidelines may have caused or contributed to the reduction in the significance of an unregistered private equity sale, relative to findings in earlier private placement studies of a positive response.

Test evidence confirms that liquidity and changes in liquidity help to describe the cross-section of market responses at private equity placement announcements. Significance is noted for both factors when the initial and the change in liquidity are considered separately. This conditioning is statistically significant at the 1% level for liquidity changes without allowance for initial liquidity levels and at the 5% level for liquidity when the change in liquidity is not included. An interactive variable for the product of liquidity and the change in liquidity is significant at the 5% level, as well. The positive market responses are strongly associated with the size of the issue and a negative response, suggested by Jensen (1986) for the initially more liquid firms, does not result for the average announcing firm. The greater significance of the change in liquidity factor is anticipated by Myers and Majluf (1984).

Firms that perform on a par with or better than the market in the weeks prior to the announcement are associated with better responses than firms that perform poorly relative to the market. Additionally, an aversion exists by the market to the firms in the sample that have very low levels of pre-offer liquidity. Overall, announcements are favored for the better-performing firms in this study's sample that are receiving larger liquidity infusions and that initially possess higher levels of liquidity. The market effectively uses recent firm performance and existing levels of liquidity as proxies for survival.

1.7 Organization of the Study

A theoretical and empirical review is provided in the next chapter. Implications for modeling and cross-sectional analyses are developed in Chapter 3. Sample selection procedures and tests to discriminate between competing hypotheses are provided. Variables are selected and tests are designed to provide insights into the explanatory power of various factors influencing market responses to private placement announcements.

Results of the tests outlined in Chapter 3 are provided in Chapter 4. The final sample is described. Additional consideration is given to the limitations of any results. Conclusions are reached. The paper closes in Chapter 5 with a summary, review of salient results and suggestions for subsequent research.

1.8 NOTES

1.   See Table 1 for a detailed description of liquidity.
2.   The selection and description of the private placement market is fully developed in Chapter 2.
3.   Smith and Kim (1994) consider the potential for the mitigation of the under-investment issue of Myers and Majluf (1984) and the free cash flow problem of Jensen (1986) by the purchase of slack-poor firms by those with excess free cash flow. Their study supports one of the main contentions of this examination - that slack has measurable value to the slack-poor firm - and provides direction on the separation of the negative effects of free cash flow and the favorable impact of available or arriving slack.
4.   A private placement is a debt or equity issue that involves no public offering; as such, the issue is commonly exempt from registration with the Securities and Exchange Commission (SEC). A review of the Securities Act of 1933, as amended through 1996, and its implications for private placements is provided in Appendix 1.
5.   See Smith (1986), Asquith and Mullins (1986 a, b) and Mikkelson and Partch (1986).
6.   For example, information concerning private placements is regularly limited and examinations of market responses to these placements is difficult. Rule 144-A and Regulation S of the SEC hold that transactions taking place directly between firms and large informed investors are exempt from the scrutiny given public offerings. These exemptions limit the occurrence and the substance of announcements by firms of private placements.

CHAPTER 2

Theoretical Development of an Optimal Liquidity Hypothesis

2.1 Outline and Objectives of Chapter Two

The theoretical and empirical encouragements for an optimal liquidity hypothesis are reviewed in this chapter. Supplementary theories complementing this hypothesis are developed. Considerations are granted to: (1) the contrast between slack and free cash flow, (2) capital and ownership structure, (3) information asymmetries and the costliness of effective signaling, and (4) the choice of private over public markets.

The slack-poor firm is confronted with a number of issues. Whether pursuing funds in the public or private markets, a decision to issue seasoned equity or new debt will have implications for the firm's capital and ownership structure and will provide a signal to the asymmetrically informed capital markets of the firm's current and future prospects. Agency costs of free cash flow may be suffered and be particularly onerous for the firm that is seen already to possess or be acquiring substantial free cash flow. A pattern exists, broadly illustrated in this chapter, of negative market responses to announcements by firms of upcoming equity issues; this pattern does not exist, on average, for private placements.[7] While traditional financial theory proposes a horizontal demand curve for a firm's security issues in a frictionless market and an independence of a firm's financing and investing decisions, recent empirics support contrasting points of view. No clear consensus exists concerning the wealth effects of private placement announcements.[8] These contrasting points of view are reviewed in the following pages.

2.2 Financial Slack, Free Cash Flow and Firm Value

Asquith and Mullins (1986 a,b) note that "an enduring anomaly in financial economics is the reliance of firms on internally generated funds" and their reluctance to issue stock. They observe an overall pattern of negative stock price responses to new equity issues.[9] Management can generally expect this non-positive market response to new security issue announcements. Asquith and Mullins find a downward-sloping demand curve for a firm's equity, on average, and reject traditional financial theory; they illustrate an overall positive market response to a company's cash outflows - in the form of dividends or stock repurchases - and negative responses to cash inflows - dividend reductions or stock sales.[10]

Johnson, Serrano and Thompson (1996) attribute the negative returns noted in prior research to consistencies in four theoretical models. These models link lower returns with adverse selection costs, lower management ownership of the firm, misuse of free cash flow or expectations of declining firm performance. Smith (1986) examines these negative stock price responses and the influence of the process of raising capital on corporate financial and investment policy. He offers several hypotheses as explanations for the negative share response.[11] Although Smith proposes that share price response may be a function of changes in expected cash flows that is an indirect effect of a slack-poor firm being provided slack, he doesn't allow specifically for a share price response to this provision of slack.

2.2.1 Financial Slack and Firm Value

Slack has value to the firm with insufficient slack. Yet, as managers consider their options in acquiring slack, they are confronted with the Myers and Majluf (1984) dilemma: Equity offering announcements may inform the market that management believes assets in place and future investment opportunities are overvalued. This implies that a new issue has a negative information effect.

Similarly, as many firms with inadequate slack are in financial distress or in a growth cycle, debt may not be a viable alternative. The firm in financial distress may be denied access to the credit markets or, if credit is available, given access to only the costliest debt.[12] If a firm is growing and suffering from inadequate slack, it is confronted with the Myers (1977) underinvestment issue; to avoid wealth transfers from shareholders to debtholders, the firm may pass up valuable investment opportunities.[13] Myers and Majluf (1984), as noted above, suggest that private placements of equity might mitigate their underinvestment issue and provide additional slack to the firm with limited internal funds.[14]

Myers and Majluf (1984) demonstrate that management forgoes profitable investment requiring external equity financing when there is a transfer of value from old to new shareholders. This underinvestment issue is alleviated if managers can costlessly convey their private information to the market.[15] To insure the credibility of the signal of firm value to investors given by the private placement, firms must bond against the resale of the stock "long enough to allow private information to become public." The credibility of the signal is also improved by the purchase of restricted stock by a single investor at a price that reflects a control premium. In this case, the financial slack, information and ownership structure hypotheses might each explain elements of the stock price response to private sale announcements. The signal might be affected by changes in ownership concentration or sales to a management buyer or stockholder.[16] Earlier research suggests that the stated purpose of the funds being acquired, such as for a "speculative product," impacts the market's response to the private placement.[17] The suitability of a private placement to provide slack to a growing firm and to influence a favorable market response for a firm with "speculative" opportunities is affirmed by Kenworthy (1993) and Myers (1992). Both studies favor private funding for "emerging growth companies."

Thus, the optimal liquidity hypothesis proposes that a more valuable signal is provided to the capital markets by the slack-poor firm than by its counterpart; the hypothesis needs to allow for mitigating factors such as investment opportunities and equity ownership. Existing studies making these sorts of allowances have been mixed in their conclusions concerning the ability of financial slack measures to explain cross-sectional relationships for firms making acquisitions or equity issues.

Pilotte (1992) considers the growth opportunities for firms arranging new financing and introduces a financial slack measure. He specifies slack as "the ratio of the sum of cash and marketable securities to total assets for the fiscal year end prior to the announcement" of new financing. He extends the intuition of Ambarish, John and Williams (1987) and Jensen (1986). Pilotte shares these other authors' premises that growth options favor the equity issues and cash accumulation does not. Yet, some of his predictions and "contrary" results seem not to favor Jensen and actually encourage a consideration of an optimal liquidity hypothesis in the context contemplated by this study. The accumulation of free cash flow is perceived negatively - on average - by the market; yet, Pilotte finds (using his slack measure as a proxy for a firm's unobservable free cash flow) security issue announcement period abnormal returns unrelated to his free cash flow proxy. The cross-section of abnormal returns observed in his sample are better explained by the firms possession of growth options. These options are associated with positive market responses to security issues. An average negative response is widely observed for all straight equity issues.

Pilotte (1992) examines a sample of firms announcing an equity, debt or convertible offering between 1963 and 1984. Growth rates of such factors as market value of equity and sales proxy for a firm's growth options. In a traditional market modeling of abnormal returns, he finds that all of his growth measures help to describe the cross-section of abnormal returns at security issue announcement. Pilotte observes overall negative returns for most security issues. These negative returns are tempered by measures of growth, capital expenditures, research and development, Tobin's Q and a price-earnings multiple. In short, the greater a firm's future observable prospects, the less negative - on average - market response to new financing announcements. None of the coefficients for his slack measure in his varied cross-sectional modelings is significant, however. Given no significance, no inference can be drawn.

The non-significance of the slack variable in Pilotte (1992) has several implications. While the author implies that his slack measure is a proxy for a firm's unobservable free cash flow, it seems more a measure of the financial slack targeted by this study. These troubling results highlight the difficulty of separating the financial slack and free cash flow hypotheses that compete for position in explaining observed returns at private placement announcement. As Pilotte notes, if his proxy is for free cash flow, then the expected coefficient is negative and significant. Yet, in five of his nine cross-sectional models, the sign is positive. In none of the modelings is the coefficient of slack significant. Modeling abnormal returns at security issue announcement as a function of growth, market-to-book value, slack and security type, the author tells a growth story. He focuses upon his other variables and grants only cursory mention to the slack coefficients in his nine cross-sectional modelings. Rather than discount the strength of a free cash flow hypothesis in explaining the cross section of issuing firm's returns, Pilotte's proxy may be compromised by its proximity to financial slack. Whereas the free cash flow hypothesis, considered in the following section, proposes an adverse wealth effect at security issue announcement, the optimal liquidity hypothesis suggests the opposite for the slack-poor firm. The measure he chooses may capture elements of both theories and thus be a "wash," as his results seem to imply.[18]

Smith and Kim (1994) provide distinctive measures for slack and free cash flow. Though the two concepts are similar, the authors are able to confirm both the value of slack and the detriment of free cash flow. Defining slack as "liquid assets and riskless borrowing capacity beyond that which is needed to meet current operating and debt servicing needs" and free cash flow as an unobservable excess cash flow over positive NPV projects, they examine acquisitions. The authors consider a sample of 827 offers between 1980 and 1986. They find that the largest total return to shareholders occurred where a free cash flow rich firm provides slack to a slack-poor target or bidder in an acquisition. This is consistent with Jensen (1986), Myers and Majluf (1984) and Lehn and Poulsen (1989).

Smith and Kim's (1994) stratification of firms according to available liquidity provides results that support their joint hypothesis concerning slack and free cash flow. While the sources of all the gains in merger activity are not understood, their work is revealing. They illustrate significantly higher returns for slack-poor firms being provided slack in an acquisition.[19] They highlight the importance of slack in the market's response to acquisitions. A similar endorsement is expected by an optimal liquidity hypothesis of the value of slack to the privately placing slack-poor firm.

Studies in the finance literature that focus upon financial slack are uncommon. It is not clear when first the concept of slack is mentioned or a measure provided in finance texts. While no reason for this dearth is immediately evident, the proximity of definitions of financial slack to descriptions of free-cash-flow may hold the key. Since the development of agency theory beginning decades ago and Jensen's (1986) seminal invitation to deeply investigate agency costs arising from free cash flow, interest has been detracted from financial slack. Thus, financial slack has at least three appeals as a research topic. First, though several differing definitions might invite review, it is observable and measurable. This contrasts with free cash flow, that is based upon an unobservable set of investment opportunities. Secondly, there is a lack of consensus on the implications of various slack measures in the studies here reviewed. And finally, optimal levels of liquidity have been extensively investigated where that level is exceeded with the accumulation of free cash flow, but much less detailed attention has been paid to the importance of slack in explaining market responses to corporate "events" for the firm with limited liquid resources.

2.2.2 *Free Cash Flow and Firm Value*

Free cash flow is liquid resources available to management in excess of those required to meet current operating and profitable investment needs. An optimal liquidity hypothesis holds that the market responds adversely to the acquisition of liquidity by a firm already possessing or, by the acquisition, preparing to possess free cash flow. Where management is given control of liquid assets in excess of those required to meet current needs and pursue shareholder wealth maximization, those liquid assets can be wasted. Shareholder interests are sacrificed as management pursues its own agenda.

Fama and Jensen (1983) examine the costs of the separation of firm ownership and control and Jensen (1986) highlights the particularly onerous agency costs that can arise from the firm's accumulation of free cash flow. Fama and Jensen suggest a corporate structure that can reduce costs of separation. The authors' proposals are intuitively appealing and lend themselves to broad empirical study, but still allow shareholder wealth losses except in the most ideal circumstance. Although authors who have succeeded the seminal examination by Berle and Means (1932) have supported contrasting views concerning the implications of separation, a substantial literature has evolved in the past decade that documents a plethora of agency costs.[20] Perhaps chief among these detractors from firm value are the costs of free cash flow.

Free cash flow is distinct from financial slack, though they occupy the same continuum. The relationship between slack and free cash flow is illustrated in Figure 1. The decreasing expected value of each additional dollar of slack is revealed along with the increasing expected cost of free cash flow as the firm accumulates liquid resources. A global minimum cost of holding liquid assets is reached beyond which those assets become free cash flow and stockholder wealth is sacrificed. This optimum exists where the marginal expected cost of accumulated excess free cash flow is equal to the marginal expected cost of inadequate financial slack. Although Figure 1 implies a symmetry and monotonic relationship between slack and free cash flow, this may not be the case and the relationship between the two certainly varies from firm to firm. Slack has value to the firm and to shareholders as the firm meets operating needs and invests in wealth increasing projects. Slack is good because it enables the firm to avoid stockout costs. Slack is observable and measurable, provided one can accept the accuracy of audited financial statements. Free cash flow is unobservable to outsiders. (Talented industry analysts may differ on this point.) Free cash flow, in the hands of a management that is unable to reveal its moral character, represents under-utilized capital and inadequate returns to investors. Free cash flow incurs carrying costs.

Jensen (1986) discusses the costs to shareholders of free cash flow and provides anecdotal evidence of the benefits of removing free cash flow from management control; he describes methods of restoring firm value through the use of debt and takeovers and detracts from the desirability of firm diversifications.[21] In an examination of firm value, cash flows and equity issues, Brous and Kini (1992) support both Jensen's (1986) free cash flow hypothesis and the cash flow signaling hypothesis of Miller and Rock (1985). The two hypotheses highlight the significance of observed cash flows and liquidity levels to firm value. The former proposes, due to such factors as management hubris and undiversified investment of human capital in the firm, a destruction of value with excess cash accumulation. The latter hypothesis holds that the adequacy of internally generated funds in the firm is signaled by costly dividend policies that preclude optimal levels of investment by the firm. The importance of liquidity (slack) to the firm and the costliness of accumulated cash flow are underscored.[22]

It is the point at which slack is accumulated and becomes free cash flow that is not easily specified. Measures here proposed, that allow for such factors as a growing firm's greater need for slack and a mature firm's slack requirements to fund common stock dividends, should begin to provide that specification. The similarities between slack and free cash flow remain. Yet, once distinctive definitions and proxies are provided for each, the financial slack and free cash flow hypotheses are examined separately. The testable implications for each premise are different in the same spirit that stock-out problems and excess carrying cost problems are different. Methodologies such as those used by Smith and Kim (1994) can serve as a starting point in providing the necessary separation.

While this study and separation do not provide the final word on these two hypotheses, the tests selected promise meaningful results. One of the gravest limitations of this study is the overlap in measures of slack and free cash flow and the polarity in the empirical implications of each. Stockholders interests are well-served by a firm with adequate slack but are defeated where that slack becomes free cash flow.

2.3 Ownership Structure, Equity Issues and Firm Value

A firm's capital structure is represented by the mix of the long-term components on the right hand side of the firm's balance sheet. Financial theory supports the irrelevance of capital structure to firm value in a frictionless and fully informed world. As successive assumptions of this classical theory are changed and as empirical studies add to our knowledge of market phenomena, the inadequacy of this theory in describing the "real" world becomes apparent. Contemporary capital structure theory includes the static trade-off model, holding that capital structure choice is based on the minimization of the firm's cost of capital, and the pecking order model; this second model suggests that the firm successively prefers internal financing, then the use of debt and finally the issue of new public or private equity to acquire capital.[23]

Extensive research has revealed relationships between a firm's selection of long term financing components and its size, industry, opportunities for growth, age, international exposure and regulatory environment. While the sources of financing in a frictionless world may have no impact on a firm's cost of capital, allowing for these frictions (such as taxes, agency costs and transaction costs) lends relevance to a firm's selection of a capital structure. However, the appropriateness of one or another mix of debt and equity securities and of leverage is not known with accuracy.

An early study by Baxter and Cragg (1970) highlights both the non-random nature of the choice of financing mix by firms and the need for a more general theory of capital structure. It holds that an optimal financial structure may exist and vary among firms, but that its exact specification is very unclear. Taub (1975) attempts to ascertain those factors that influence capital structure and decisions by management to issue debt or equity, either publicly or privately. He extends Baxter and Cragg, finding that firm security choice does not necessarily accord "with what might be expected." While extensive investigations have ensued concerning a firm's move to some presumed optimal capital structure, Taub's call for a more general theory of capital structure portends much of the dissension addressed in this review. Since his work in the mid-1970's, theory and evidence have provided support for opposing theories encouraging and discouraging different levels of ownership concentration and varied financial and dividend policies.[24]

Since Taub's work, the sources of wealth losses in new public equity issues have been described in the framework of six general hypotheses. Diltz, Lockwood, and Min (1992) consider the "size, tax, agency cost, bankruptcy, target debt ratio and asymmetric information hypotheses." Their findings support the premise that issue size and information asymmetries drive wealth losses at equity issue announcements. Acknowledging the existence of frictions such as taxes, transaction costs, agency costs and asymmetries of information, firms are presumed to pursue some optimal capital and ownership structure. They are further assumed to be maximizing shareholder wealth. Towards these ends, firms make financing choices and may select private markets to serve their financing needs.

Ownership structure includes both the mix of equity-type securities and the levels of "inside" and "outside" ownership. Theory exists that favors inside ownership to the extent it aligns management with shareholder interests, but not to the extent that inside ownership allows or encourages management entrenchment and expropriation of stockholder wealth.

The ownership structure hypothesis implies that market re-evaluations of the firm following private placements of equity are the result of anticipated changes in managerial performance. Systematic patterns have been observed in the selection of capital and ownership structures among firms based on such factors as age, size and industry.[25] Company choice of ownership structure impacts firm value, but - in the "real world" - theory cannot unambiguously predict the impact on firm value of changes in ownership structure or of a firm's decision to issue equity.

Berle and Means (1932) propose that dispersed ownership allows self-interested management to deploy corporate assets for their own benefit; pursuing personal and not shareholder welfare, managers of the publicly held corporation invest in their own human capital and not necessarily in the maximization of shareholder wealth. Jensen and Meckling (1976) note that, given this cost of separation, an optimal level of outside funding and mix of outside debt and outside equity evolve that result in an optimal capital structure. They note that the separation is by design; it is endogenous. They highlight the importance of management ownership and of contractual cash payments (such as those for debt and, to a lesser degree, for dividends) to bond management and mitigate agency costs.

Demsetz (1983) responds that the stock and human capital markets exist to monitor management behavior. He remarks that "it is foolish to believe that owners of valuable resources systematically relinquish control to managers who are not guided to serve their interests." He suggests that there is no relation between ownership structure and corporate performance. Easterbrook (1984) comments in a similar vein on the importance of capital markets in monitoring management. Easterbrook notes the existence of agency problems between management and shareholders. He endorses the value of monitoring by the capital markets and proposes that generous dividend policies be designed to minimize the sum of agency, tax and capital market costs. He suggests that these policies force the firm regularly into the capital markets to be revalued. Demsetz and Lehn (1985) find no significant relationship between ownership concentration and accounting profit rates. They cast doubt on the Berle and Means (1932) thesis. They treat "ownership concentration as an equilibrium response to a firm's operating characteristics."[26] Findings by McConnell and Servaes (1990) contrast with Demsetz and Lehn. They find that corporate value is associated with the structure of equity ownership. Equity issues generally alter the size and class of inside equity ownership. These issues alter both sides of a firm's balance sheet and preclude an "uncontaminated" laboratory in which to examine conflicting theories of capital and ownership structure. Nonetheless, numerous studies examine the wealth effects of equity issues and changes in a firm's capital structure.

Stulz (1988) shows how management control of voting rights affects firm value; this value "depends critically on the distribution of votes between management and outside shareholders." He proposes that managerial control of the firm favors firm value at lower levels of ownership to a greater extent than at high levels. He shows how management control of voting rights affects firm value and how this control can impact financing policies.[27] McConnell and Servaes (1990) provide broad support to Stulz's premises. Their findings are inconsistent with Demsetz (1983) and Demsetz and Lehn (1985).[28] McConnell and Servaes hold that corporate value is impacted by the structure of equity ownership and they imply that valuation effects at private placement announcements will be impacted by the type of purchaser.

Stulz's (1988) premise is that firm value is positively related to management ownership at low levels and negatively at high levels. This is not entirely consistent with findings by Morck, Shleifer and Vishny (1988). They note that "theoretical relationships alone cannot unambiguously predict the relationship between management ownership and the market valuation of a firm's shares." This has implications for the impact on ownership structure of a firm issuing equity privately; the new equity affects the firm's capital and ownership structures.[29,30]

An examination of inside ownership, outside blockholders and employee stock ownership plans (ESOPs) is conducted by Park and Song (1995). They find that firms with ESOPs outperform those without ESOPs overall, but that this outperformance is a function of the "efficiency" of the firms ownership structure and effective outside monitoring. Similar to Holderness and Sheehan (1988), they stress the importance of outside blockholders to monitor a potentially entrenched management. For the firm placing equity privately, the desirability of the placement to an entrenched management favors an ESOP where management retains voting rights. Yet, if this retention does not favor shareholder wealth, a sale to an ESOP to encourage employee alignment with shareholder interests or to an outside blockholder to encourage monitoring might be preferred.

Brickley, Lease and Smith (1988) find that entrenched managements defer equity placements to maintain control or place equity privately to insiders to further increase their power. Harris and Raviv highlight the potential of a friendly buyer being part of a resistance strategy by a management valuing control.[31] Institutional owners or purchasers illustrate a pattern of siding with management in a takeover by demanding a higher premium (that favors all shareholders) or by resisting the sale. A private placement of equity to one of these institutional blockholders could have the a) effect of increasing shareholder wealth in a successful merger, of b) further entrenching management friendly to the private placement buyer or c) better monitoring a management, either entrenched or not, independent of takeover activity. The work by Brickley, Lease and Smith is endorsed by Raad and Ryan (1995), who document similar relationships between tender offer success and ownership in a sample of 1984–1991 tender offers. Barclay and Holderness (1989) (extending results that favor the impacts of corporate raiders on firm value in Holderness and Sheehan, 1983) also provide evidence of the value of control in their examination of block trades of outstanding equity.[32]

McConnell and Servaes (1995) study the relationships between ownership structure and capital structure for firms with varied levels of growth options. They examine the interactions between corporate value, leverage and equity ownership. Queuing firm value to Tobin's Q as the dependent variable, they consider a sample of firms between 1976 and 1988. They discover a non-linear relationship between inside ownership and firm value; this is consistent with McConnell and Servaes (1990), Morck, Shleifer and Vishny (1988) and Stulz (1988).[33] The gist of their work is that, concurrent with varying levels of inside ownership, debt can have "both a positive and a negative effect on firm value because of its influence on investment decisions." Debt is favored for those firms with fewer growth options.[34] A conjecture develops that the private placement of equity is favored for firms with more growth options. This effect is expected to vary by the firm's available slack, the informativeness of the private purchasers action and existing inside ownership.

Much of the work by McConnell and Servaes (1995) supports earlier work by Bagnani, Milonas, Saunders and Travlos (1994). They consider inside ownership, management risk aversion and the return premia on the firm's debt. Their underlying premise is that with increasing inside ownership comes an increasing aversion to risk with higher levels of undiversified management investment in the firm. Examining a sample of firms between 1977 and 1985, they find a non-monotonic relationship between managerial ownership and bond premia (risk aversion). Bagnani, et al discover an incentive by managers to expropriate bondholder wealth in favor of stockholders at low levels of managerial ownership (less than 5%). They find a "positive relation between managerial ownership and bond return premia" in the median range (5% to 25%), as well. Above 25% ownership levels, however, they find managers protecting their own undiversifiable human capital with an increase in management risk aversion and a reduction in bond return premia; these incentives for "wealth-transferring activities are reduced at higher managerial ownership levels." Supporting the step-wise regressions of Morck, Shleifer, and Vishny (1988) and Wruck (1989) - considered in depth below - their findings outline one of the implications of private placements. Given a management or friendly-to-management purchase of a private placement, wealth transfers to bondholders may occur. Similarly, with a non-management and outside purchaser, there is an implication that there will be a wealth transfer from bondholders; this is true especially at higher levels of inside ownership.

At lower levels of inside ownership, the placement better aligns management interests with shareholder interests, increasing firm value. There may be a point of inflection in the 20%–30% effective insider ownership range above which management risk aversion detracts from shareholder value. Ownership above 5% and below the 20–30% range leads to varying degrees of entrenchment and a possible sacrifice of firm value, as well.[35] Given these troublesome premises, the impact of a private placement upon insider ownership may be clear, but - with current evidence - impact on firm value is not.

Wruck (1989) uses an analytical framework based on "a broad academic literature linking ownership concentration and firm value" and finds that private sales of equity generally increase inside ownership concentration. Her evidence is consistent with changes in ownership concentration revealing new information to the market about firm value or about the future allocation of corporate resources.[36] She proposes that private sales of equity provide the opportunity to examine the effect on firm value of changes in equity ownership concentration.

Examining 99 private placements by NYSE and AMEX firms between 1979 and 1985, she observes an overall positive abnormal return, on average, of 4.5% upon announcement of private placements. Voting rights sold average 19.6%. Her results contrast with the negative abnormal returns generally observed after public sales of equity. Changes in firm value are strongly correlated with changes in ownership concentration. Increases in firm value are observed at lower (less than 5%) levels of inside ownership concentration and at higher levels (over 25%), as well. A less significant inverse relationship is observed between increases in ownership concentration and firm value at middle levels of inside ownership (between 5 and 25%). Her analysis provides an empirical link between the market response to these placements and changes in ownership concentration.

The sample used by Wruck (1989) is split between registered and unregistered private placements of equity. Among the primary appeals of private placement is the frequent circumnavigation of onerous floatation costs. These costs include SEC filings and costs of registration. Inasmuch as unregistered securities are restricted and cannot be easily resold, the willingness of a substantial investor to assume an illiquid equity position signals a belief by the investor in the investment.[37] This information release is magnified, given Wruck's purchases averaged close to 20% of voting rights, by an intention by private purchasers to monitor and assist firm management given the long-term ownership normally required with unregistered and restricted securities.

The importance of unregistered securities to explanations of anomalous market response to private placement announcements has been both highlighted and compromised since her study. Work by Ferreira and Brooks (1999) uses registered private placement announcements. Yet, their sample - particularly the ones that illustrate the most favorable market responses to the announcement - is populated by firms that, on average, go out of business. The importance of restricted and unregistered placements in Wruck's (1989) sample is implied. However, since her work, the SEC has relaxed trading restrictions on unregistered securities. Sales of these privately placed securities may occur between informed and "sophisticated" investors.[38] Thus, the costliness of the restricted securities to the initial investor is reduced since the sale of these securities is now possible despite the restrictions. As well, the informativeness of the purchase to outside investors is reduced given successively more generous SEC guidelines.

The stock price response to private placement announcements observed by Wruck (1989) provides a measure of the overall average increase in wealth experienced by nonparticipating shareholders as a result of the sale. Her findings include significant positive abnormal returns for several months prior to each announcement. She observes few sales to managers or to parties they control and negative returns after sales to management-controlled shareholders. She suggests that observed private placement discounts are "compensation for expert advice or monitoring services provided" by the private investors. Most of the buyers (75%) in her sample assume active roles as managers or directors after their purchase. She makes no separable allowance for the firm's access to slack. Professor Wruck observes the average positive performance following privately placing firms' announcements and attributes the pattern to improvements in ownership structure.[39]

It is clear that changes in ownership structure impact market responses to private placement announcements. But, the simultaneous roles played by a firm's available slack, its capital structure and capital spending programs and by the resolution of information asymmetries are not immediately evident.

2.4 Information Asymmetries, Equity Issues and Firm Value

An "information release" hypothesis may displace others in explaining negative average returns observed at the announcement of public equity issues. The information hypothesis holds that changes in equity value upon announcement of private placements of equity are driven by shifts in the market's assessment of existing asset values and future opportunities, and claims on the firms assets by various stakeholders. This hypothesis also helps to explain the anomalous returns for privately placing firms.[40] Miller and Rock (1985) and Myers and Majluf (1984) provide theories, based on the resolution of information asymmetries, predicting negative responses to seasoned equity offerings as a function of reduced cash flow expectations and management signaling of firm overvaluation, respectively. Their theories are contrasted with the positive abnormal returns observed, on average, at private placement announcements.

Akerlof (1970) provides an early study of the costs of asymmetrically informed markets. Unless management is able to apprise investors of favorable opportunities available to the firm and of the value of the firm's existing assets, a fair value transaction will not take place. The market breaks down. Management is often hamstrung in selecting a costly signal to inform investors of current firm value and firm prospects. Studies suggest debt levels (Ross, 1977), entrepreneurial inside ownership (Leland and Pyle, 1977; Stulz,1988; and Jensen and Meckling, 1976) and dividend payments (Miller and Rock, 1985) as appropriate signals of inside information to outsiders. Extensive empirics have evolved that lend some support to each of these signals.

According to Ross (1977), for a signal to be valid it must be costly and observable.[41] Ross drops the fully informed and frictionless markets assumptions of classical capital structure theory and develops an "incentive-signaling" model of managerial incentives and capital structure that serve as signals to an asymmetrically informed market. He ultimately endorses the costliness and efficacy of leverage to signal firm value, but leaves open the possibility that many other costly and observable signals exist. Private placements are costly to management in terms of discounts generally offered to buyers and the loss of control often given to the purchaser. The placements become observable upon announcement.

As such, and in conjunction with other financing decisions, the placements may play a crucial role in providing a "signaling equilibrium" to the capital markets. Leland and Pyle (1977) note that numerous markets are characterized by information asymmetries between buyers and sellers and that without information transfers, markets perform poorly. This has implications for sales of equity to inside and outside investors. Miller and Rock (1985) respond to these implications and hold that debt or equity placement announcements convey the information that expected levels of "internally generated funds" (a proxy for available slack) have been overstated; this implies that new issues will have a negative impact on firm value proportional to the size of the offering. Conversely, if the market is already aware of a firm's lack of liquid resources, an optimal liquidity hypothesis suggests a favorable market response to the announcement of arriving liquidity.

The information theory mentioned here is extended to equity issues in an "information-theoretic" model by Lucas and McDonald (1990). They report several observations concerning new equity issues: (1) equity issues are generally preceded by positive abnormal returns in the firm's stock, (2) these issues are normally preceded by an overall rise in the market and (3) stock prices drop, on average, upon new equity issue announcements.[42]

A paper by Ambarish, John and Williams (1987) generalizes the results of Miller and Rock (1985) and Myers and Majluf (1984). It proposes that insiders convey information in many costly ways. The authors of this 1987 study suggest negative announcement effects for firms disclosing "private information primarily about assets in place" and positive effects for firms disclosing "information primarily about opportunities to invest." Insiders convey information and construct an "efficient signaling equilibrium" with such tools as dividends, new investment and net new issues of common stock. Dividends are seen as an inefficient signal. An efficient signal conveys the desired information with minimal dissipative costs. In order to maximize shareholder wealth among all possible separating equilibria, management needs to construct a signal that combines the three tools above.[43]

Private placements, therefore, cannot be considered separately from other corporate financial policies. The placement has effects other than the resolution of information asymmetries and the value of the private placement signal needs to be measured in the context of other concurrent signals. The announcement of a private placement does provide a costly signal to the marketplace of a firm's financing decision. But, whether the firm is attempting to reveal current asset values or future prospects, the signal's effect is tied to other disclosures such as a capital spending plan or the identity of the purchaser. A multitude of other factors, such as management ownership levels, the company's liquidity and profitability and macro-economic conditions impact the signal's effect, as well.

Masulis and Korwar (1986) consider the information and ownership structure implications of new equity issues. They observe an overall negative stock price response to announcements of underwritten (public) common stock issues; this implies a conveyance of negative information by the offering.[44] Their results are consistent with the Jensen and Meckling (1976) and Leland and Pyle (1977) models. Dierkens (1991) examines "the relevance of information asymmetry between the managers of the firm and the market for the [public] equity issue process." Developing four proxies for information asymmetry, she tests for the interaction of these proxies with equity issues.[45] She shows that increases in information asymmetries significantly increase the negative market response to an equity issue announcement.

Information asymmetries contribute much to the costliness of the traditional capital markets. Brennan and Kraus (1987) describe conditions under which the adverse-selection problem, founded on these asymmetries, may lead to the sacrifice of a profitable investment due to the costliness of financing. They model the theoretical framework within which "efficient financing" is accomplished and do not specifically allow for private placements. Their theory may, however, provide some rationale for the positive abnormal returns often observed at private placement announcements. In order to avoid wealth transfers from old to new stockholders, a private sale is made to an "informed" investor. Funds are acquired and a simultaneous favorable signal to the outside markets is provided.

Bayless and Diltz (1991) also consider the impact of asymmetric information on the financing decisions of management and support the main premises of Myers and Majluf (1984). They recognize the importance of slack in influencing management's decisions concerning security issues. They do not address the role that might be played by the private markets in resolving the Myers and Majluf (1984) underinvestment issue, nor do they consider the role slack might play in characterizing returns upon public or private issue announcement.

Diamond (1985) provides a model that gives a policy of disclosure that makes all shareholders "better off than no disclosure." Normally, firms aren't in the business of buying or selling their own stock, so they must convince ongoing investors that any nonpurchase is not a signal that the price is too high. He builds a theory of optimal information release where the firm represents a "natural coalition for maximizing the welfare of its security holders." A literal interpretation of his results precludes the actions taken by security analysts, but firms, according to the author, "release somewhat less information than the model predicts." His results apply to information that analysts could have acquired at some finite cost anyway, but his work still stresses the importance of the costly resolution of information asymmetries. The equilibrium effects of his model favor the intuition of Ross (1977) and highlight the costliness of existing asymmetries to the firm and its security holders.

Private placement announcements and the anomalous response of markets to those announcements need to be considered in the context of a firm's other financial disclosure policies. Similar to Dierkens (1991), where a market is particularly uninformed about a company due to its size, analyst scrutiny or trading activity, any financial disclosure may invite extreme market response. The returns on a firm's stock following a private placement announcement deserve particular scrutiny for the firm about which the market is "uninformed."

An accounting literature considers the impact of firm financial disclosure policies on stock prices. Healy and Palepu (1993) summarize the key ideas of accounting information models. They confirm that conflicts of interest can exist between management and shareholders and that a need exists for verifiable "audited" information. If a firm has established a pattern of accurately reporting its activities to shareholders and other outsiders, "unexpected" announcements may be more believable and market response, if the information is positive, more favorable. A firm of this type can announce a private placement and an intention to invest proceeds in some valuable growth option and expect a positive market response. A firm that hasn't established this "trustworthy" pattern cannot rationally expect rapid market acceptance of unforeseen financial disclosures.

In a context similar to that of Healy and Palepu (1993), Mann and Sicherman (1991) tie market response to equity issue announcements to "management reputation." If management has established a pattern of non-diversifying acquisitions - desirable for shareholders at the expense of risking the undiversified human capital of management - markets respond more favorably to equity issue disclosures. Extending this, the firm issuing equity privately, that has a record of non-diversifying acquisitions, might expect an even more positive market response than the average for private placement announcements. Importantly, however, these might also be the firms that are more likely to go out of business in the longer term horizon examined by Ferreira and Brooks (1999).

Frankel, McNichols and Wilson (1995) examine firm discretionary disclosure policies and link them to external financing decisions. They hold that "firms attempt to mitigate potential consequences of differential information through disclosure" and that firms that more frequently issue capital tend to issue more financial disclosures. An earlier study by McConnell and Muscarella (1985) shares a similar intuition. They hold that managers seek to maximize firm value with their capital expenditure decisions and to reveal information about these decisions towards that end. Management has a measurable incentive to reduce information asymmetries such that general cash offerings are more favorably received.

Private placements might also be a solution to a fear of potential litigation that often accompanies a later declining value in a seasoned equity issue. Legal restraints preclude a firm issuing an optimistic report near the time of an equity issue, but a private placement may still protect the firm from legal liability.

Healy and Palepu (1990) examine adjusted changes in earnings per share and report no "systematic decrease in earnings following a new equity issue announcement." Their results, broadly consistent with Myers and Majluf (1984), imply that managers issue equity and reduce leverage when they foresee an increase in business risk. Investors recognize management's superior information and revise asset and equity betas upward; this explains negative average stock price responses. Hansen and Crutchley (1990), on the other hand, document a significant decrease in earnings, on average, following new equity issues by a firm. They hold that offerings are motivated by earnings downturns.

In addition to an information release hypothesis, Kalay and Shimrat (1987) test the power of price-pressure and wealth-redistribution hypotheses in explaining negative market responses to seasoned equity issues. The former hypothesis maintains that "firms face a downward sloping demand curve for their stock" and the latter holds that bondholders gain from equity issues at the expense of stockholders. Although all three hypotheses predict an unfavorable impact on stock prices, their study examines the response of bond prices to the announcement of equity issues. The authors' findings suggest that equity issues convey negative information about the entire firm's prospects and not just the value of equity. This provides more definition to the anomalous nature of the average positive responses of markets to private placement announcements.[46]

Private placement announcement effects include an amelioration of information asymmetries. This amelioration may be augmented by an announcement of the intended use of the funds received. Whether for capital expenditures, acquisition or debt service, market response will vary. The use of private placement proceeds for bank debt repayment, for example, could depress stock value. Successive examinations by James (1987), on the uniqueness and informativeness of bank loans, and by Hull (1994), on the negative signaling impact of bank loan reductions, encourage an allowance for the purpose of private placements, especially where that purpose includes debt reduction.

Hertzel and Smith (1993) consider the discounts granted buyers of private placements of equity and attribute changes in firm value upon announcement of these sales to resolutions of information asymmetries *and* the anticipated effects of changes in ownership structure. They extend the Myers and Majluf (1984) model to allow for the assessment by private placement purchasers of firm value through their negotiations with management. They hold that investor "willingness to invest, together with management's desire to forego" a public issue, conveys management's belief that the firm is undervalued. They develop tests to discriminate between information and ownership structure (monitoring) effects.

Hertzel and Smith (1993) use a sample of primarily smaller NASDAQ and OTC firms issuing privately between 1980 and 1987. They confirm and extend Wruck (1989) by finding that, in addition to ownership structure effects, private sales of equity have important and positive information effects.[47] The authors find that information effects are more important for their smaller and less scrutinized firms than are any ownership structure effects. They examine the discounts offered private placement purchasers. Hertzel and Smith find an average discount of 20% off the market price of equity is given to private placement purchasers in their sample. The largest sized placements relative to outstanding equity are associated with the highest abnormal returns at announcement.

Despite this discount and a revelation to the market that a substantial relative portion of a firm's equity has traded (private placements in their sample averaged over 15% of outstanding equity value for the firm) below market, positive abnormal returns are observed. Whether the discount offered to buyers is compensation for becoming informed about a firm placing privately, as the authors claim, or may simply reflect a higher required rate of return for the buyer, is not immediately clear. Hertzel and Smith (1993) comment on the "growing and illiquid" nature of their sample, yet they make no specific allowance for the correlation between available slack and market responses to private equity placements. The authors confirm the desirability of private placements to firms in financial distress, the high underwriting costs of public issues (averaging over 5%), and the greater discount offered by "riskier" firms. Firms broadly underperform markets prior to the private placements. The authors conduct cross-sectional tests of the two competing hypotheses and provide results that are consistent with Morck, Shleifer and Vishny (1988). The "ownership effects are less important for smaller firms" than larger firms in examinations of ownership structure.

The predictions of the information and ownership structure hypotheses considered in the Hertzel and Smith (1993) sample are similar. Their analysis and support for the former hypothesis is based on the premise that the information effects should be larger where the potential degree of undervaluation is high. Their assumption is that the potential degree of undervaluation is greater for their smaller and less intensively scrutinized sample.

For these smaller firms, the ownership structure hypothesis is not entirely discounted, but the information effects seem to dominate.

2.5 Security and Market Choice and Firm Value

Introductory courses in finance and accounting suggest a firm's matching of long term assets with long term debt or equity financing. No specific prediction evolves from this premise for the choice of long term debt or equity funding for a given long term asset.[48] However, a few generalizations can safely be made: following some presumed purchase of start-up equity, a standard of mortgage financing for real-estate, bank floor plans for inventory and intermediate term loans for equipment, is suggested. A firm's choice of capital structure has proven much more complex in theoretical developments and empirical examinations. Varied hypotheses have been offered to describe a firm's selection of its capital structure. Myers (1993) considers the firm's "search for an optimal capital structure" and discusses the subjective appeal of static-trade-off, pecking order and organizational hypotheses. His quest for a "general theory of capital structure choice" is frustrated by the countervailing forces influencing a firm's security choice.

Investigations of the impact upon outstanding security values, pursuant to new debt or seasoned equity offerings, generally provide some insights into capital structure theory. Yet, these insights are often cloudy and encouragements for a firm's choice of debt or equity security are unclear. It is in this realm that the slack-poor firm makes a security choice and determines whether to issue publicly or privately.

2.5.1 Security Choice and Firm Value

Bayless and Diltz (1994) consider capital structure theory and examine the firm's choice of debt or common equity issues. They examine "a large sample of public security offerings" between 1974 and 1983. They find equity is costly to most firms because of information asymmetries and that debt is discouraged for "riskier" companies.[49] They are unable to support traditional capital structure theories that imply target leverage ratios and that incorporate the tax advantages of debt. They support a pecking order hypothesis. Firms first prefer internal financing and secondly, debt.

Higher stock prices encourage equity issues. Larger issues are more frequently debt. Consistent with Ross (1977) and Leland and Pyle (1977), they find the most profitable firms are more likely to issue debt. Favorable overall market performance encourages equity issues; this is consistent with Brous (1992) and Lucas and McDonald (1990). Debt is issued in periods following a fall in interest rates.

While a firm's selection of debt or equity is uncertain, Bayless and Diltz (1994) develop a model that incorporates the factors above and correctly classifies 80 percent of the issues in their sample. No specific allowance is made for slack or free cash flow, but the bond suggested by Ross (1977) for high cash flow firms is illustrated by those firm's higher debt issues. The greater probability of equity issue for the less profitable firms implies an equity issue for the slack-poor firm.[50] As in Marsh (1982), highly significant differences exist between debt and equity issuers.[51] The works by Marsh, later refined by Bayless and Diltz, provide a modeling that a financial manager might be able to use in selecting first an equity or debt issue and, later, whether to issue publicly or privately.

Sant and Ferris (1994) consider three primary influences for the financial manager issuing equity. These are the capital structure, price pressure and negative information hypotheses.[52] Sant and Ferris examine equity issues by all equity firms, thus controlling implications of the capital structure hypothesis, and generate results that support Miller and Rock (1985) and Myers and Majluf (1984). The issue's effect is "driven by changes in the expectation of future cash flows." The effect is tempered by expectations of the issue in the marketplace. Schadler and Moore (1992) consider this topic and find that investors "usually anticipate a debt issue" and use a firm's financial characteristics to "increase their expectation" of a stock issue.

Myers and Majluf (1984) assume that managers do not own or transact in a firm's shares. Their simultaneous premises that slack has value and that market responses to seasoned equity issues will generally be adverse, are compromised by this omission. Bradford (1987) makes this allowance on Myers' and Majluf's behalf. He extends the intuition of Jensen and Meckling (1976) that a level of inside ownership develops endogenously for the firm that is optimal for the firm, and develops a theoretical model.[53] Management ownership - both buying and selling - has implications for the issue decision. Management ownership is generally favored, but insider sales or an entrenched management can exacerbate negative market reaction to issue announcement.

Bayless and Diltz (1991) consider the effects of information asymmetries on security choice. They provide "strong" support for the proposals of Myers and Majluf (1984). They find debt issues positively related to levels of available slack and to firm size; the overlap of a free cash flow premise of a debt bond and of the suitability of debt for larger and better known firms becomes apparent.

Brennan and Kraus (1987) and Asquith and Mullins (1986b) remind the researcher of the interrelatedness of the factors influencing security choice and market response to issue announcements. Brennan and Kraus propose that the most efficient financing may involve simultaneous security retirements, equity issues and convertible offerings. Thus, in order to acquire slack and provide the firm with financial resources to pursue its investment agenda at minimal cost, many factors are involved. The firm is providing signals simultaneously with its dividend policies, investment disclosures, ownership structure, stock repurchases, management compensation policies and security issues.[54]

2.5.2 Private Market Selection and Implications for Firm Value

The suitability of a private placement over a public issue of equity is sometimes immediately evident for a given firm. Firm characteristics may boldly dictate the greater cost of a public issue or the "perfect" fit provided only by a private placement.[55] For smaller and emerging growth companies, private placements can provide an ideal fit. Degrees of disclosure and speed of market penetration vary from state to state, but private placements often provide capital when other sources are unavailable.[56,57]

The private markets have come into greater favor.[58] Private financing offers flexible financing without the regulatory and underwriting expenses found with most public issues. It provides a potentially lower cost of capital. Sherman (1991) notes that the typically larger and more sophisticated buyer of a private vs. public placement allows a more complex and confidential transaction to take place. Stevens (1988) remarks on the avoidance of many flotation costs, provision of funds to obscure companies, the speed of funds provision and the maintenance of a privately held firm as distinct advantages for this market.[59]

Lerner (1994) finds that private transactions can more quickly avail the firm of the talents and funds from venture capitalists in times of depressed equity values. Lerner further allows that these "seasoned venture capitalists" are later more proficient at taking companies public when equity values are high. The private markets allow the firm to avoid costly market frictions and access "customized" financing.

Firms find it necessary - absent an available shelf registration - to maintain sufficient reserves, or financial slack, to pursue positive net present value options as they arise. The firms are confronted with being penalized for the over-accumulation of financial slack to the point where it becomes free cash flow and for the under-accumulation of financial slack to the point where favorable opportunities are foregone. Myers and Majluf (1984) propose that private equity sales may mitigate this underinvestment issue. The underinvestment dilemma arises when a profitable investment opportunity is abandoned due to an expectation that existing shareholder wealth will be reduced as the market responds negatively to a public equity issue announcement.[60]

In the Myers and Majluf (1984) paradigm, firms forego value-enhancing projects because of issues of adverse selection, information asymmetries and agency costs. A fear exists among prospective public placement purchasers that a self-serving management will provide new security buyers only the "good news"; these prospective purchasers believe that managers will waste liquid firm assets upon unstated and shareholder wealth-sacrificing but management-serving objectives. These purchaser fears result in a loss in security value as the new issue is sold. The expected loss to existing shareholders - or bondholders in the case of Myers (1977) - outweighs the gain they might have enjoyed from pursuing the profitable investment option. Myers and Majluf's main message is that firms suffering from insufficient slack increase their value by acquiring more. The private equity placement may deliver needed slack without the costly reduction in existing shareholder wealth that commonly arises with a public equity issue.[61]

Stevens (1988) provides one of the earlier outlines of the desirability of private placements. The firm with limited needs or that wishes to remain private may desire the private markets or may have no other choice. An unknown company is able to avoid unfavorable information releases.[62] Stevens notes that the troubled firm more easily acquires much needed slack in the private markets. The often onerous costs of public issues are avoided. Melnik and Plaut (1995) model a positioning of the public and private debt markets based on degrees of information asymmetry. A firm less well known and of higher default risk is seen to place privately. Companies choose a public or private market depending on the lowest "cost" of borrowing. Melnik and Plaut are able to tie the expansion of the private markets to regulatory frictions, but their theory is primarily descriptive and of only limited use to the manager choosing markets. They emphasize the roles of information asymmetries and of transaction costs in dictating private market selection.

Blackwell and Kidwell (1988) examine cost differences between public and private placements of debt.[63] They propose that firms make their issue decision based purely upon which market offers the lowest costs of issuing securities. They examine a sample of over 200 debt issues between 1979 and 1983. (Fewer than one fifth of these were private.) The authors suggest that firms choose whichever market provides the lowest "yield on net proceeds." Yet, they make no real allowance for the impact of a public or private issue on existing security holders. Their predicted transaction costs analysis does not provide for the contrasting wealth losses of private versus public issues. Their results have intuitive appeal as the smaller and less well known firms issue privately.

2.6 Firm Liquidity and Market Response to Private Equity Placement Announcements

From these discussions develops a supplement to existing theory and an optimal liquidity hypothesis. While a broad literature has evolved that considers the implications of changes in capital and ownership structure, and a related school has extensively examined the information content of sundry debt and equity issue announcements, no known study provides the extensions of this examination.[64] As noted in the introduction and in its simplest form, the theoretical supplement merely proposes that slack has value and is a critical component of management's decision to issue and of the market's response to the announcement of a private placement of equity. The basic premise is that this response is characterized by a firm's access to slack and that markets favor the slack-poor firm. The market is expected to penalize the firm that is believed to possess or be acquiring free cash flow.

The theory provides testable predictions that slack will help to describe the cross-section of market returns subsequent to any security issue announcement. The hypothesis suggests that included slack proxies in a modeling of market responses to security issues will assist management in predicting the consequences of a new issue. The nature of the issue and firm specific characteristics will favor a public or private placement.

In the examinations that follow, several hypotheses explain elements of the observed results. For example, the empirical predictions of the information, ownership structure and optimal liquidity hypotheses are qualitatively similar. With an "improvement" in a slack-poor firm's ownership structure at private placement along with a positive information release that placement proceeds will be used to fund some growth opportunity, all three theories help to explain positive expected returns. The free cash flow hypothesis describes negative market responses to a private placement by a free cash flow rich firm. A neutral average market response to a private placement announcement is explained in part by both an optimal liquidity and a free cash flow hypothesis; the firm may be acquiring needed slack and inviting a positive stock price reaction while concurrently accumulating excess free cash flow and neutralizing the positive response that might have been preserved with a smaller placement. Tests are designed and variables are selected in Chapter 3 to help distinguish between these main hypotheses.

2.7 NOTES

7. See Wruck (1989), Hertzel and Smith (1993) and Fields and Mais (1991) for evidence of overall favorable market reactions to private equity-type security issue announcements.

8. An examination by Ferreira and Brooks (1999), for example, finds that positive wealth effects observed at the announcement of registered private placements are later sacrificed by firms that go out of business. The registered securities and the insider selling prevalent in their sample may explain much of this contrast, but their results beg review.

9. There are only two widely observed exceptions to the "norm" of negative abnormal returns upon announcement of equity financing. In the first exception, Schipper and Smith (1986) observe an "average increase in shareholder wealth" upon announcement of equity carve outs. They attribute this anomalous return profile to the separation of known subsidiary growth opportunities from the greater information asymmetries that would be suffered by an offering of seasoned parent equity. The second exception is the market response to announcements of private placements of equity-type securities.

10. Examinations by Masulis and Korwar (1986) and Smith (1986) also find that public offers of equity-related issues are associated with significant negative stock price responses. Asquith and Mullins (1986 a,b) make no separable allowance for slack.

11. These include movements away from an optimal capital structure, expectations of the issue, changes in expected cash flows, information effects and ownership structure effects.

12. The value of slack to the firm in financial distress is suggested by Lummer and McConnell (1989) and Gilson, John and Lang (1990), who observe significant positive abnormal returns for firms in financial distress being granted troubled loan renewals and private debt restructurings, respectively. Their findings suggest not only a favorable signal to investors of the troubled firm's future prospects, but also of the value to the troubled firm of available credit and improved credit terms - indirect measures of slack.

13. With his "theory of corporate borrowing," Myers (1977) suggests that the amount of corporate borrowing is inversely related to the portion of firm value made up by these real options. The growing firm is discouraged from providing liquidity through the use of debt. According to Myers, a firm whose value is made up disproportionately of growth options - the implied case with much of the Hertzel and Smith (1993) private placement sample - finds much of its value is made up of discretionary future investments.

14. Huberman (1984) illustrates the dynamic of a firm's choice of liquidity levels and provides indirect theoretical support for Myers and Majluf (1984).

15. An addendum to and extension of Myers and Majluf (1984) is provided by Viswanath (1993). He extends the Myers-Majluf model for the firm that faces "unacceptable dilution" in the future from the issue of equity. That firm may violate the pecking order hypothesis favored by Myers and Majluf and issue equity to finance a current investment. This

doesn't necessarily signal firm overvaluation, as Myers and Majluf imply. It may merely illustrate management's desire to acquire less costly funds via equity issue today versus a greater loss to equity value that may occur with a future equity issue. Several of Viswanath's model's other predictions are consistent with empirical observations. Even a slack-rich firm might favor an equity issue to generate cash if the firm expects a costlier issue in the future.

16.   See Barclay and Holderness (1989) and Holderness and Sheehan (1988).

17.   Denis (1994), however, notes that investment opportunities do not "necessarily" influence positive market responses. The interplay of these opportunities with financial slack and private placements is not, however, clear.

18.   Ang (1991) remarks on corporate slack and confirms that while slack has value, its impact on corporate value is often indeterminate. In a similar vein, Beranek, Cornwell and Choi (1995) broadly define financial slack and find market response to long term financing improves with capital expenditures and suffers with increasing slack. In other words, the market favors external financing by the firm that is slack-poor and has visible growth opportunities. External financing by slack-rich firms is penalized.

19.   The Smith and Kim (1994) findings are extended and supported by Bugeja and Walter (1995). They find that the provision of financial slack to a slack deficient target "is associated with a significantly higher premium" in takeover activity.

20.   See, for example, Vogt (1994), Perfect, Peterson and Peterson (1995), Johnson, Serrano and Thompson (1996) Bayless and Chaplinsky (1996), Cornett and Tehranian (1994) and Smith and Kim (1994) for recent discussion of the implications of Jensen's (1986) study and Myers and Majluf's (1984) predictions.

21.   Portfolio theory describes the benefits of diversification for the individual or institutional investor. Studies such as one by Mann and Sicherman (1991) remind management that its duty is to focus its expertise on some core business and leave the benefits of risk reduction through diversification to its shareholders.

22.   Other studies too numerous to list here have documented the agency costs of free cash flow in many varied environments. Studies that dispute those costs are being challenged by authors such as Perfect, Peterson and Peterson (1995) in their study of self-tender offers.

23.   Examining the impact of corporate holdings of liquidity on firm value, a recent paper by Opler, Pinkowitz, Stulz, and Williamson (1999)

contains evidence supporting the static tradeoff model; another study by Shyam-Sunder and Myers (1999) provides evidence generally supporting the pecking order model. The infusion of liquidity from equity private placements could represent either the generation of required financial slack with the pecking order model or a return toward optimal liquidity, when liquidity poor, with the static tradeoff model.

24.   The value of slack to the slack-poor firm is illustrated by Myers and Majluf (1984) and the costliness of acquiring slack in "traditional" fashions is confirmed in a broad literature that has developed over the past decade. Loderer, Sheehan and Kadlec (1991) observe underpricing of new equity issues, presumably to entice investors, and Speiss and Affleck-Graves (1995) illustrate the average long-run underperformance for firms issuing seasoned equity. Firms are observed suffering costly initial and seasoned issues and are seen to underperform, if they offer seasoned equity, even in the long run. Bhagat, Brickley and Lease (1986) provide a contrasting undercurrent to these later studies. They find that the authorization of additional common stock, that is a precursor to later issues, provides mixed results. While a stock issue may be expected to signal management's belief in firm overvaluation, the stock authorizations in their sample are not followed by significant negative returns; this is probably because the prevalent uses by industrial firms in their sample of the authorized shares are for stock dividends and splits.

25.   See Smith and Watts (1992) for an illustration of trends in financing, dividend and compensation policies among firms with varied growth options and degrees of regulation and size. They review patterns in corporate financing policy as a function of these factors and the ability of a contracting hypothesis to explain corporate policy decisions. A firm's selection of overall capital structure is related to firm value, but relationships are not always clear. Hull (1994), in a "pure" capital structure examination, illustrates a positive correlation between firm value and leverage, but acknowledgès a number of "discrepancies" confirmed in prior and subsequent research.

26.   See Jensen and Warner (1988).

27.   Stulz (1988) ignores information asymmetries. His study emphasizes the costliness of management resistance to takeover offers as their control of voting rights increases. However, a "powerful" management, that believes the firm is undervalued, may recognize this asymmetry and be acting in shareholder interests by resisting offers.

28.   Fields and Mais (1994) also support Stulz (1988). They examine the relationships between management ownership and market responses to

seasoned equity issues. Their results reveal a "significant negative relationship" between announcement period abnormal returns and "changes in management ownership and the level of management ownership." They discount the influence of outside blockholders and variables intended to capture the information content of the seasoned public equity issue announcements.

29.   McConnell and Servaes' (1990) findings are not consistent with Morck, Shleifer and Vishny (1988) at insider ownership levels above 5%, but are broadly consistent with Stulz (1988).

30.   Findings by McConnell and Servaes (1990) - of increases in firm value with increasing levels of institutional ownership - extend earlier results by Mikkelson and Ruback (1985), who show that a shift to more concentrated holdings of stock by non-managers is associated generally with increases in firm value.

31.   Varma and Szewczyk (1993) suggest no continuing pattern of management use of private placements to further entrench themselves "at the expense of current. . . . shareholders." Their examination of purchases of private placements of bank equity suggests that "buyers of privately placed common stock provide a monitoring service that aligns the interests of the bank's managers and shareholders." Their findings support an ownership structure hypothesis.

32.   Evidence is presented by Amihud, Lev and Travlos (1990), who find that "corporate insiders who value control" are unlikely to issue new equity. They find higher managerial ownership associated with a lower probability of new equity issues in acquisitions.

33.   A great deal of theoretical and empirical research considers relationships between insider control of the firm and firm value. Non-linear relationships are encouraged in much of the research, with increasing management ownership favoring firm value at lower levels of ownership and leading to management entrenchment and risk aversion (decreasing firm value) at higher levels.

34.   The desirability of debt for firms with available cash flows and limited growth options is supported by Myers (1977) and Smith and Watts (1992).

35.   Testable implications are developed and step-wise regressions are provided for these contrasting premises in Chapter 3.

36.   Her observed stock price responses to private equity placement announcements favors the non-monotonic results of Morck, Shleifer and Vishny (1988).

37. Appendix 1 reveals that these unregistered equity purchasers may be much more liquid now, however, than before 1990.

38. Davis (1990) and Milligan (1990) describe the incentive to trade in the private placement market under the relaxed guidelines of Rule 144-A. The new rule allows institutions holding at least $100 million in stocks and/or bonds to "trade among themselves without first registering the [privately procured] securities with the SEC or holding them for two years. The goal is the creation of a liquid institutional market for debt and equity that would take its place next to existing retail and traditional private placement markets."

39. Recent studies by Loughran and Ritter (1995) and by Bayless and Chaplinsky (1996) affirm the dilemma found by firms issuing equity. The long run underperformance of the average equity issue between 1970 and 1990 and the expectation by management of adverse market responses to equity issues are considered in these studies, respectively. While the latter study proposes a "window of opportunity for seasoned equity issues," that results from periodic reduced information asymmetries, it doesn't consider the desirability of a private placement to the slack-poor firm.

40. See Kalay and Shimrat (1987). Fields and Mais (1991) reject tax and ownership structure hypotheses in their examination of the announcement effect of privately placed convertible debt; they support an information hypothesis as explaining the positive average effects of these announcements.

41. The costliness of information conveyance is one of the factors influencing the underinvestment issue of Myer and Majluf (1984), as well.

42. This theory supports earlier work by Mikkelson and Partch (1986) who hold that management offers debt or equity when, in management's view, securities are overpriced. Later studies by Brous (1992) endorse Lucas and McDonald's (1990) theory.

43. Asquith and Mullins (1986 a,b) provide empirical support to the premise that capital market response to new equity issues is related to three corporate financial policies. Dividends, stock repurchases and equity issues are seen as signals by outsiders of "management's appraisal of the firm's future cash flows." Cash outflows from the firm are generally viewed positively and inflows, negatively.

44. It is the voluntary nature of the equity issue and not the equity issue in-and-of-itself that seems to lead to a market re-evaluation of the firm's stock. An examination of voluntary versus involuntary stock issues by commercial banks (See Cornett and Tehranian, 1994) finds significantly

greater stock declines with voluntary and not regulatory capital acquisition issues. Managements' willingness to issue stock and the subsequently greater "voluntary" decline is consistent with Ross (1977).

45. Dierkens' (1991) proxies for information asymmetry are: (1) stock market reactions to earnings announcements, (2) the residual variance of the issuing firm's daily stock returns, (3) the number of public announcements in a given period for the firm, and (4) the trading "intensity" of the firm's stock.

46. Doran (1994) finds that in addition to regular financial disclosures and financing decisions, stock splits - an event that results only in a simple note to a firm's statement and has no tangible effect on cost - are used by management to reduce information asymmetry, signal future earnings and attract analyst attention.

47. Fields and Mais (1991) examine positive abnormal returns associated with private placements of convertible debt. They conclude, similar to Hertzel and Smith (1993), that these private placements mitigate an information asymmetry. They contrast their findings with negative average abnormal returns observed with public sales of convertible debt securities.

48. Beranek, Cornwell and Choi (1995) examine a large sample of firms between 1971 and 1988 and generate results that support a premise of matching long term assets and long term liabilities. Their findings also encourage a preference for internal over external financing. Of particular note, the firms with greater financial slack are observed pursuing less external financing in the period following the slack measurement. The converse is implied and intuitive; slack-poor firms require more external financing.

49. Studies of new debt issues generally provide less significant results than those of equity issues. Examinations by Sun (1995) and Kolodny and Suhler (1988) illustrate this outcome. The former study reveals a marginally significant negative wealth effect for announcements of new debt issues. Greater effect size is observed for larger issues. The latter study reviews the non-significance of results often encountered in debt studies. In that work, Kolodny and Suhler discount wealth transfer and asymmetric information hypotheses and find no significant impact of new debt issues upon existing equity holders in general. They are able to partition their sample and reveal a favorable market response to firms investing in R&D or reducing nonsystematic risk, however.

50. Bayless and Diltz (1994) build upon the earlier results of Marsh (1982). He confirms that companies are "heavily influenced by market conditions" and actually do have some target debt ratio in mind.

51. Myers (1977) suggests the use of debt by firms with fewer growth options, as an agency cost of debt is an underinvestment in growth options. This is inconsistent with findings by Sun (1995) of a more favorable response to debt issues for firms with greater R&D expenditures; this difference highlights the frequent contrast between offered capital structure theory and empirical observations.

52. Barclay and Litzenberger (1988) hold that these three issues inadequately describe market responses to security issues. They propose that much of observed market responses are the result of a rebalancing of portfolios. The firm's equity holders suffer the transaction costs incurred by investors as they buy and sell the firm's stock; the stock loses appeal to some investors and increases for others. Barclay and Litzenberger submit that these investors "charge" the existing equity holders for the transaction costs of rebalancing.

53. His findings show that "a statistically significant portion" of all the equity issues in prior studies had non-negative share price responses to issue announcements.

54. These policies and disclosures may also be enacted sequentially to maximize investor or manager value. Sant and Thiewes (1995) are consider such sequencing in a study of stock splits and equity issues.

55. Sherman (1991) and Andrew Myers (1992) discuss the reduced transaction costs and exemption from many SEC registration and reporting requirements - that appeal to many firms with a particular set of capital needs - provided by the private markets. The unregistered share has specific empirical implications considered in Chapter Three.

56. See Tucker (1994) for a review of the focus of private placements and their advantages for many firms.

57. Degrees of disclosure, varied security regulations from state to state and the speed of market penetration in private vs. public markets is a point of contention in many financial and legal circles. See Sherman (1991), for example, for a discussion of these issues.

58. The *Federal Reserve Bulletin* reports that close to $100 billion were gathered privately in the new securities market in each of the four years through 1995. Amounts issued privately have stabilized after peaking several years ago.

59. Smith (1991) echoes a belief in the vitality of the private market as private interests are securitized and traded despite registration restrictions. Provided the trades are between informed investors and are otherwise exempt from SEC scrutiny, such as between large international investors, they are allowed under the new rules. Yorks (1990) and Tucker

(1994) predict increased private financing activity domestically and globally.

60.   This recalls the underinvestment issue of Myers (1977), where a firm with valuable "growth options" and insufficient capital to fund these investment opportunities will forego the issuance of risky debt.

61.   Many firms are not slack-poor in an immediate sense, but have inadequate slack to fund valuable growth options. Two exceptions to the Myers and Majluf underinvestment dilemma are when the value of assets in place is known or when a growth option is sufficiently valuable to offset the cost of issuing underpriced equity - although in this second case there is still an agency cost and system loss. The private markets may be able to provide needed slack without the need for these exceptions. The provision of slack along with favorable information releases or an improved ownership structure, should be positively received by the market.

62.   Varma and Szewczyk (1993) find that the resolution of information asymmetries appear to be the driving force behind bank decisions to issue equity privately. Their results do not support a suggestion that insiders place equity privately to further entrench themselves. Instead, and consistent with Wruck (1989), the privately placed equity serves not only as an information release but also as a monitoring service to better align management with outside shareholders.

63.   Costs of informing the public and meeting SEC guidelines for a public issue generally far outweigh the savings to the firm in a customized private issue of less than $10 million. (See Kenworthy, 1993).

64.   Carey, Prouse, Rea and Udell (1994) note that few major studies of the private placement market have been conducted and that "only a few articles have appeared in economics and finance journals" since 1972.

CHAPTER 3

Examinations of the Optimal Liquidity Hypothesis

3.1 Outline and Objectives of Chapter Three

The primary objective of the study is to determine whether the evidence supports theoretical models holding that slack creation can be wealth-enhancing. The secondary objectives are to broadly explain the sources of wealth changes at the announcements of private placements of equity. Methodologies are developed in the following pages towards achieving those objectives.

This chapter is organized as follows: The empirical model is described in the next section; dependent and explanatory variables are introduced; proxies for liquidity, growth options and ownership structure as they relate to an optimal liquidity hypothesis are considered successively in Sections 3.3 through 3.5; a set of control and interactive variables are defined in Sections 3.6 and 3.7; the sample selection procedure is provided in Section 3.8 and statistical concerns with the data and its selection are discussed; the limitations of the selected methodologies are examined as the chapter closes.

3.2 Development of the Empirical Model

3.2.1 Theoretical Development of the Model

Figure 1 illustrates the theory motivating the empirical tests. Variables pertinent to the optimal liquidity hypothesis are motivated by the relationships represented in Figure 1. Firm value is first enhanced in Figure 1 by additional liquidity as it allows the firm to avoid costly external financing. Myers and Majluf (1984) and Miller and Orr (1966, 1968) suggest this enhancement is very important for the firm with valuable growth options and for avoiding "stockout" costs, respectively. Firm value, however, according to Jensen (1986) and Stulz (1990), eventually falls with increased liquidity with the accumulation of the agency costs of excess free cash flow. At the point at which the expected marginal benefits of additional liquidity equal the marginal costs of free cash flow, the firm has reached its liquidity optimum.[65]

Thus, as a first approximation, the value (stock price of the unlevered firm) of the firm can be expressed as:

$$Stock\ Price = b_0 + b_1(L - L^*)^2 \tag{1}$$

where L is the firm's liquidity level, b_0 is a constant and b_1 is the coefficient of the squared difference between a firm's liquidity and its optimal level of liquidity, L^*.[66] A positive sign is expected for b_0 and a negative sign for b_1. Given that these signs occur, an optimum exists where $L = L^*$.

The first derivative of Equation 1 with respect to liquidity specifies the impact of a liquidity change on stock price. Allowing for discrete changes in liquidity in Equation 1 yields:

$$\Delta(SP) = (2b_1L - 2b_1L^*)\Delta L \tag{2}$$

which implies that a stock price (SP) change due to a change in liquidity depends upon (1) the change in liquidity and (2) the difference between existing and optimal liquidity levels. In general terms:

$$SP\ Effect_{i,t} = f[initial\ liquidity,\ liquidity\ change,$$
$$optimal\ liquidity\ level]_{i,t} \tag{3}$$

Referencing Figure 1, the stock price impact for firm "i" in period "t" is a function of the firm's movement along the x-axis, where with inadequate liquidity the market rewards the additional liquidity up to the point where the slopes of the expected benefits of additional slack and costs of free cash flow are equal. The optimal level of liquidity varies from firm to firm. It depends upon the discretion and reputation of the firm's management, proxied in this study by the firm's ownership structure. It depends also upon its access to growth options and other factors such as the degree to which the firm is scrutinized by the investing public. Optimal liquidity is expressed as:

$$L^*_{i,t} = f[\text{ownership structure (discretion), growth options}]_{i,t} \quad (4)$$

A growing firm (as inFigure 2) or a firm with an entrenched management (as inFigure 3) has more and less of an optimal level of liquidity - respectively - relative to its counterpart.[67] Substituting this linear model for optimal liquidity (L^*) into Equation 2 yields:

$$\Delta(SP) = [2b_1L - 2b_1(b_2g + b_3s)]\Delta L \quad (5)$$

where g is "growth options" and s is "ownership structure." From Equation 2, b_1 is expected to be negative and is assumed not to be trivial. Since growth options favor the accumulation of liquidity, b_2 is expected to be positive; b_3 varies depending upon the composition and concentration of inside ownership. An entrenched management increasing its discretion with a private placement results in a negative-signed estimate of b_3, whereas a purchase by a "trusted" and well-monitored management results in a positive-signed estimate of this parameter. Expanding Equation 5 provides:

$$\Delta(SP) = 2b_1L\Delta L - 2b_1b_2g\Delta L - 2b_1b_3s\Delta L \quad (6)$$

Dividing both sides of Equation 6 by 2 gives the expression:

$$\Delta(SP)' = b_1L\Delta L - b_2^*g\Delta L + b_3^*s\Delta L \quad (7)$$

In Equation 7, b_1 is expected to be negative as before, $b_2^* = -(b_1b_2)$ and is expected to be positive and $b_3^* = -(b_1b_3)$ and is indeterminate, as b_3 varies depending on the nature of any inside ownership. The change in stock price is a function of the firm's existing liquidity, the change in liquidity, growth options and ownership structure. Firm value is enhanced by arriving liquidity when there are greater growth options. Firm value is either enhanced or reduced by additional liquidity depending upon the composition of the firm's ownership.

Equation 7 is modified to provide a testable empirical model for the studies that follow. Dividing the left and right hand sides of Equation 7 by the change in liquidity (ΔL) provides:

$$\frac{\Delta(SP)'}{\Delta L} = b_1 L + b_2^* g + b_3^* s \qquad (8)$$

Equation 8 provides also for a set of "other factors"; these are proxied by the control variables described below. Measures of the dependent and explanatory variables in Equation 8 allow the testing of an optimal liquidity hypothesis. The ideal circumstance is, however, unavailable. Optimal liquidity levels, for example, are unobservable and can only be implied. Proxies for the factors in Equation 8 can be selected, however, to provide a suitable forum for testing.

3.2.2 Empirical Development of the Model

To test the model in Equation 8, stock price reactions to private placement announcements are examined. The private placement announcement is a liquidity enhancing event with desirable empirical features. Rather than the market "guessing" at the information release in a public equity issue announcement, the private placement buyer clearly signals his or her belief in any "hidden" firm value with the size and price of his or her purchase. An adjusted measure forwarded by Wruck (1989) allows for the examination of the portion of the return that is due to factors other than information asymmetry resolutions. This significant encumbrance in separating factors affecting wealth effects faced by the investigator of public equity issue announcements is avoided.

3.2.2.1 Specification of the Dependent Variable

A dependent variable is constructed with abnormal returns measured in two ways. The first measure is the traditional abnormal return for the issuing firm over the period from 3 days before the announcement to the day of the announcement, if there is time to trade an announcing firm's stock on the announcement date. For firms announcing after the close of trading, the first trading day after the announcement is treated as day 0. This initial measure is calculated as:

$$AR_{i,t} = R_{i,t} - \left[\hat{\alpha}_i + \hat{\beta}_i(R_{m,t})\right] \qquad (9)$$

where $AR_{i,t}$ is the abnormal return for firm i in period t, $R_{i,t}$ is the total return for firm i in period t, and $\left[\hat{\alpha}_i + \hat{\beta}_i(R_{m,t})\right]$ is the market-model predicted return for firm i in period t; $\hat{\alpha}_i$ is the intercept for security i predicted from the pre-event estimation period from day −200 to day −60; $\hat{\beta}_i$ is the slope coefficient of security i over this same pre-event estimation period and $R_{m,t}$ is the value-weighted return of the market during period t.

The second measure is the adjusted abnormal return employed as the dependent variable in this study:

$$AR_{i,tADJ} = [1/(1-\gamma)][AR_{i,t}] + [\gamma/(1-\gamma)]\,[(P_b - P_0)/P_b] \qquad (10)$$

where $AR_{i,tADJ}$ is the adjusted abnormal stock return for firm i in period t, γ is the ratio of shares placed to shares outstanding after the placement for firm i[68], and $AR_{i,t}$ is the traditional measure of the abnormal return for firm i in period t described above. P_b is the market price two days prior to the event window (taken from the CRSP files), and P_0 is the placement price. The element $[(P_b - P_0)/P_b]$ is the discount received by the private placement purchaser.[69]

The placement price is taken from the private placement announcement. The unadjusted abnormal stock return is measured for selected event windows between days −59 and 10. The estimation period for the parameters of the model providing the adjusted returns measures is the same as that for the unadjusted measure; similarly, a four-day announcement period is selected for cross-sectional study from day -3 to day 0.[70, 71]

3.2.2.2 *Specification of the Independent Variables*

Assuming the examination of a stock's pre- and post-announcement parameters reveals that adjusted abnormal returns are the result of some enhancement of the firm's cash flows, varied theories predict stock price changes based upon a set of descriptive independent variables. These variables are described in the following pages, employed in Equation 11 and listed in Table 1. Equation 11 is estimated to test Equation 8:

$$AR_{i,tADJ}/\Delta L = B_0 + B_1 \text{ (Earnings/Price)} + B_2 \text{ (New Product)} \quad (11)$$

$$+ B_3 \text{ (Working Capital)} + B_{4-6} \text{ (Single/Foreign/Mgt Investor)}$$

$$+ B_{7-9} \text{ (S Level 1-3)} + B_{10-11} \text{ (Liquidity/Liquidity Change)}$$

$$+ B_{12} \text{ (Fin. Dist.)} + B_{13} \text{ (Restricted Shares)} + B_{14} \text{ (Retire Debt)}$$

$$+ B_{15} \text{ (Prior Underperformance)} + B_{16} \text{ (Firm Size)} + \varepsilon_{i,t}$$

where $AR_{i,tADJ}$ is the adjusted abnormal returns measure from Equation 10, ΔL is the change in liquidity resulting from the private placement, B_0 is an intercept term, $B_{1..16}$ are the coefficients for the independent variables and $\varepsilon_{i,t}$ is an error term. Dependent and independent variables in Equation 11 proxy for the factors in Equation 8. Supplementing those proxies for Equation 8 factors are a set of control variables justified in prior studies of private placement announcement market reactions. Expected coefficient signs for each of the variables are outlined in the following pages. Initial study is made of the returns "normalized" by the change in liquidity as in the dependent variable in Equation 11.

An empirical dilemma develops. Authors of prior theory suggest the use of the dependent variable as developed in Equation 11. A first set of unreported tests employs this dependent variable. A positive and significant intercept is associated in those tests with 16 negative and insignificant independent variables. A more intuitively appealing model adopted by this study uses the adjusted abnormal return as the dependent variable in all reported cross-sectional analyses, absent any division by the change in liquidity.

3.2.3 Linearity of Changes in Firm Value in the Explanatory Variables

Use of Equation 11 presumes that changes in firm value at private placement announcement are linear in the explanatory variables. However, and deferring to Figure 1, it is possible that firm value is not linear in the proxies for the optimal liquidity hypothesis. Whether or not the firm value function is quadratic in the explanatory variables and thus linear in the adjusted abnormal return is not immediately clear. This empirical malady, depending upon the significance of tests for higher powered liquidity coefficients, may justify a later search for changes in the signs of liquidity coefficients for the average privately placing firm.[72]

3.3 Proxies for Liquidity in Tests of an Optimal Liquidity Hypothesis

The optimal liquidity hypothesis portrayed in Equation 8 suggests a response by the market to private placement announcements that is inversely related, on average, to a firm's available liquidity before the effects of the private placement. Even if one assumes firms do not know how to optimize their selected levels of liquid assets and are "groping around in the dark" in their choice of slack levels, the firm value curve in Figure 1 can be developed through cross-firm observations on firm value and liquidity; a similar locus of marginal costs/benefits can be traced out - as in Figures 2a and 2b or 3a and 3b - by observing changes in firm value and liquidity.[73]

Whether or not the firms are aware of their relative needs for liquidity is not a grave concern. The only necessary conditions for the meaningfulness of this study's methodologies are that (1) both the firm's existing and arriving liquidity - as a result of the private placement - are observable to the investor and (2) the investor characterizes his or her purchase decision in part as a function of a firm's possession of and need for financial slack or liquidity.

3.3.1 Liquidity/Change in Liquidity

"Liquidity" is required to explain the change in stock price in Equation 8. It is proxied in Equation 11 by liquid assets divided by funds required for current debt, operating and preferred dividend needs. The "change in liquidity" is the arithmetic difference between a firm's liquidity measure before and after the private placement. *Ceteris paribus,* a negative sign is predicted for the relation between a firm's available liquidity and the price reaction to the private placement announcement.

Theory cannot predict market responses to the change in liquidity absent knowledge of the firm's liquidity optimum. As the firm possesses a greater and greater amount of liquidity prior to the announcement, a less and less positive market response to the private placement announcement is expected. Beyond the firm's optimum, a negative response to the change in liquidity is expected. To the left of the firm's optimum in Figure 1, and the greater the relative size of the placement, the more positive is the expectation of the market's response to the placement until the liquidity provided by the placement becomes free cash flow to the right of the optimum.

3.4 Proxies for Growth Options in Tests of an Optimal Liquidity Hypothesis

3.4.1 *Earnings/Price*

Growth opportunities in Equation 8 are proxied in Equation 11 by the ratio of earnings per share to market price per share five days before the announcement of the private placement. A low earnings/price measure indicates greater growth options. This inverse measure allows firms with small positive or negative earnings to be classified similarly.[74] A negative sign is predicted by an optimal liquidity hypothesis for this inverse factor. This is consistent with Equation 8, where a positive market response is associated with increasing growth options.[75]

Motivation for this variable is represented by Figure 2. The reduced costliness of the accumulation of free cash flow and the desirability of available slack is illustrated for the growing firm with an optimal level of liquidity at L**. Smith and Kim (1994) suggest that this growth opportunities measure captures the relative importance of current to expected future cash flows. That position can be debated. On average, though, the smaller the ratio, the greater the importance of future cash flow to the firm's value and the greater the need for slack in anticipation of growth. An analogy is the higher price-earnings multiple (the inverse of this earnings-price ratio) observed for firms in growing vs. mature industries.

3.4.2 *New Product*

An empirical prediction of Equation 11 is a positive sign for a "new product" investment variable, as it proxies for an important growth option in Equation 8. Cooney and Kalay (1993) consider the potential for equity issue announcements being positively received by the markets if the announcements are coupled with proposals to increase capital expenditures. They note that a firm's capital spending plans enhance stock value, but this gain is generally overwhelmed by other factors in a public equity issue.[76] The response to a firm both placing equity privately and announcing favorable capital expenditure programs is not specifically addressed in earlier studies.

3.4.3 Working Capital

"Working capital" is required to fund the growth options of Equation 8. Similar to, but distinct from, the funding of a new product by the firm with its arriving liquid resources, is the funding of continuing operations through the establishment or replenishment of working capital. The accounting literature describes working capital as the sum of current assets and net working capital as the difference between current assets and current liabilities. Given a signaling by the firm of its inadequate slack through the announcement of a funding of working capital with placement proceeds, Equation 11 predicts a positive market response.[77] A firm is treated as funding working capital if it discloses an intention to fund working capital, continuing operations, or cash shortages or if it uses any language which implies the funding of day-to-day activities with the placement proceeds.

3.5 Proxies for Ownership Structure in Tests of an Optimal Liquidity Hypothesis

The market's perception of the discretion of the firm's management impacts its response to a liquidity infusion for the firm. Abnormal returns observed at the announcement of the placements partially reflect expectations of improved or diminished monitoring and increased or decreased discretion by management. Measures of managerial discretion are implemented in this study using a set of ownership structure proxies. These proxies provide a measure of the impact on stock price, given an increase in liquidity, relative to a firm's ownership structure. The ownership factors in Equation 11 proxy for the influence of ownership structure in

Equation 8. A significantly reduced role is expected to be played by an ownership structure hypothesis in explaining market responses to announcements by the smaller firms in this study's final sample. For the smaller and less frequently announcing firm that is covered much less in the financial press - a pattern expected for the smaller firms in this study's final sample - the "news" of the event itself and not adjacent changes in ownership structure is expected to dominate.

3.5.1 Ownership Concentration Level 1

Given the earlier findings of non-monotonic valuation impacts for the firm with increases in management ownership concentration, dummies for ownership concentration levels between 0 and 5%, between 5% and 25%, and over 25% are specified. Levels of inside ownership are taken from *Compaq Disclosure* for the reporting periods most recently available before the placement. Levels of ownership beneficially controlled by management and less than 5% of outstanding shares are not included in this measure, as they are not reported.

Positive stock price reactions upon announcement of private placements are expected for increases in the low levels of ownership prior to the private placement. An increase in ownership concentration can better align management with shareholder interests, encourage more effective monitoring of managerial performance, or increase the probability of takeovers.[78] The first ownership concentration level is a dummy for firms whose ownership concentration after the placement is 5% or less.[79]

3.5.2 Ownership Concentration Level 2

Conversely, increasing ownership concentration reduces firm value by precluding a takeover or encouraging the mismanagement of corporate resources (see Fama and Jensen, 1983). To capture this effect, an "ownership concentration level 2" variable is specified for increases in the relative ownership of managers, directors, and stockholders owning over 5% of the outstanding stock, but less than 25% after the placement. A negative impact is expected for "ownership concentration level 2."

3.5.3 Ownership Concentration Level 3

A favorable or insignificant valuation impact is expected given increases in the highest ownership concentration variable. The favorable impact is expected to be less than that for ownership concentration level 1. The third ownership concentration level is a dummy equal to one for firms whose ownership concentration after the placement is 25% or more. A positive and insignificant coefficient is expected for the variable "ownership concentration level 3."

3.5.4 Management Buyer

The sign and significance of the "management buyer" variable is a function, in large part, of the concentration levels considered above. A buyer is considered a management buyer if a manager or director or buyer friendly to management is specified in the text of the private placement announcement. A buyer is considered friendly to management if language in the private placement announcement includes reference to management's endorsement of purchase and/or purchaser. A buyer friendly to a management that owns little or none of the firm's stock better aligns management with shareholders' interests; this would imply - for lower levels of management ownership - a positive sign for the management buyer.[80] Yet an ownership structure that already includes substantial management ownership is adversely affected - from the market's perspective -by additional ownership and potential entrenchment. Here, the predicted sign for a "management buyer" would be negative.

3.5.5 Management Seller

A negative signal is implied where a sale by management accompanies the private placement; management is assumed to provide a signal of firm overvaluation where it is selling its interest. A management sale is presumed to be taking place where such sale is announced in the text of the private placement. Johnson, Serrano and Thompson (1996) support a joint signal to the markets of firm prospects with insider sales occurring prior to equity issue announcements. Management selling prior to an issue announcement is perceived perniciously by the markets. "Management seller" captures this effect and is expected to be negative.[81]

3.5.6 Single/Foreign Investor

A "single/foreign investor" exists if the private placement announcement specifies an individual/foreigner as the sole purchaser of the privately placed equity-type security. This variable allows a discrimination between the information and ownership structure effects of private placements. Monitoring is presumed to be more likely and a more favorable market response is expected with the single/foreign investor than with multiple investors.[82]

3.5.7 Retire Debt

Where funds are acquired by the firm to retire debt, a negative average market response is expected. A negative coefficient is predicted by the optimal liquidity hypothesis for the firm announcing an intention to reduce debt with the private placement proceeds.[83] A similar prediction is provided by the free cash flow hypothesis. When a valued monitor of management and a cash flow *from* the firm is reduced, the market can be expected generally to respond adversely.

A debt reduction could, however, improve shareholder wealth. If the firm is encumbered by costly and onerous debt provisions, slack is provided and costs of capital lowered by reducing this cumbersome debt. This retirement might be received favorably by the markets. Absent a retirement of such debt, an average negative response to debt reductions is anticipated.

3.6 Testable Implications of Controls for Information Releases Related to Firm Size, Performance and the Nature of the Securities Issued

A set of control variables are used in prior studies of private placements; these factors control for elements of market responses not addressed by the liquidity, growth and ownership variables adopted above. Dierkens (1991) shows that the stocks of smaller and less scrutinized firms respond more negatively than do larger firm stocks to equity-issue announcements; she finds that increases in information *asymmetry* are generally associated with significantly greater decreases in stock price.[84] The information release that is the focus of this section is *not* one related to the resolution of any information asymmetry; the impact of any resolution of an information asymmetry is captured by the adjustments of Equation 10.

The buyer provides the market with at least two types of information; the first is the revelation of inside or asymmetric information by way of the size and price of the placement; a second element of information is revealed by the nature and timing of the purchase. In other words, the buyer reveals discovered "old" information - the resolution of an information asymmetry - and also provides the market with "new" information. It is this second new information element that is addressed and whose power is proxied by the variables selected below.

3.6.1 Prior Underperformance

A more positive information effect is expected when the potential for undervaluation prior to the placement is greater. This variable is favored by Myers and Majluf (1984). A firm is considered an "under performer" if it exhibits returns over the event period (−59, −10) below the average for the value-weighted index.[85] A bias may arise if most of the firms in the sample are underperformers.

3.6.2 Firm Size

The information effect is expected to be inversely related to "firm size." A negative coefficient is expected for this variable; a greater positive average information effect is expected for the smaller firm. Firm size is also related to ownership structure, as the smaller firms in this study's final sample are expected to be associated with a reduced ability of an ownership factor to describe stock price behavior.

3.6.3 Restricted Shares (Unregistered Shares)

A more favorable information effect is expected and a positive sign is predicted for the coefficient of "restricted shares." Given the preclusion of opportunistic resale through the issuance of restricted or unregistered shares, a more credible signal and more favorable market response to restricted than unrestricted shares is expected. There is also an ownership effect. The restricted shareholder is motivated to aid the monitoring and management of the firm to insure the continuing value of his or her illiquid investment.[86]

3.6.4 Financial Distress

"Financial distress" is employed in this study to denote the presumably greater needs for liquidity by the distressed firm. This factor can also proxy for the distance of the firm from its liquidity optimum. It is a control variable suggested by Hertzel and Smith (1993) in their study of private placements. It is proxied by a firm's two consecutive prior years of negative earnings. The financially distressed firm is portrayed, on average, by a point to the left of the optimal level of liquidity in Figure 1. An increase in firm value in excess of the costs of additional slack is expected to accompany the firm's accumulation of liquidity and financial slack.

A caveat is in order. The assumption here is that the financially distressed firm can implicitly make better use of slack than its undistressed counterpart; this is not necessarily the case. For example, firms that are poorly managed and/or in a declining industry often "should" be encouraged - often against management's wishes - to cease operations and return any remaining value to shareholders. A period of financial distress can generally be expected to precede these firms' desired exits if management has been resisting those exits. If a private placement is part of this resistance strategy, the market is expected to discount firm value since management is merely denying the inevitable and is being afforded additional opportunity by the private placement to further waste corporate resources in negative NPV investments.

3.7 Interaction of the Explanatory Variables

The interaction of several of the explanatory variables are exhibited in the development of Equation 8.

3.7.1 Product of Liquidity and the Change in Liquidity

Among the first factors developed in the system of equations is the product of liquidity and the change in liquidity in Equations 5–7. A simple empirical model, examined in the next chapter, employs three factors including this product, a growth options factor and a variable for ownership structure.

3.7.2 Liquidity Squared

A factor squaring a firm's liquidity measure can test for the significance of the higher powered liquidity factor and the existence of a liquidity optimum. If there is a single liquidity optimum and the function describing that optimum is quadratic, then the first derivative of the function will be positive and the second derivative will be negative. If these signs are confirmed in empirical tests, then an optimum is implied.

3.8 Sample Selection Procedure

A sample of 543 private placement announcements is selected based upon certain key words found in a search on the *Business News Wire*. These data are first gathered using combinations of the key words "private placement," "private offering," "private stock purchase," "private purchase," "private sale" and "private stake." The announcements occur between January 1, 1988 and December 31, 1995. The date of the first announcement on this wire service is treated as day 0 in subsequent examinations unless the announcement occurs after the close of trading; the first available trading day is selected as day 0 for announcements occurring after the close of trading. The *Business News Wire* is published on the west coast and each announcement is posted in Pacific time. Observations reported after 1:00 PM Pacific (4:00 PM Eastern) are treated as occurring on the following trading day. Since the *Business News Wire* operates on days when the market is closed, any announcement occurring on closed days is treated as occurring on the next available trading day.

Only publicly-traded domestic firms are retained in the sample. The potential for the compromise of foreign firm returns by unknown or undiscovered foreign announcements precludes their inclusion. Observations are retained if sufficient stock return data is available on the CRSP tapes and if timely filings of required financial data are available on the *Compustat* tapes and *Compaq Disclosure*. Stock return data is insufficient if the stock did not trade on at least one of the days in the primary event window (−3, 0) and stocks not trading on at least on at least one of these days are deleted from the sample. Data are also considered insufficient if observations of relevant variables - defined explicitly in Table 1 - are missing from the *Compustat* and *Compaq Disclosure* files.

Many of the firms in the sample are small and have incomplete data in the computer files. Rather than force a large-firm bias (that occurs with the exclusion of smaller and less diligently filing firms) on the sample, exclusions of sample firms with available CRSP data but unavailable *Compustat* or *Compaq Disclosure* data are handled on a case-by-case basis.[87] Announcements are deleted if the type of security issued is not clear in the announcement or if the announcement is merely of a private placement "hope" and no buyer has come forward or purchase date established.

The initial observations include common stock, convertible preferred stock and convertible debt, new classes of voting and non-voting and registered and unregistered stock. The final sample is restricted to registered and unregistered common stock. Equity-type private placements announced simultaneously with debt issues are not dropped from the sample if the equity portion of the placement exceeds the debt placement and there are no other financing activities announced.

Multiple issues by single firms are handled separately provided the announcements of each issue clearly describe the private placements as independent events. Successive announcements of the partial completions of a single private placement are dropped from the sample. The earliest available announcement date is adopted for each observation.

The requirements above substantially reduce the sample size from the original 543 announcements; 240 of the announcements include only cursory mention of private placements in the past or as part of a broad financial strategy and are dropped from the sample. The *Business News Wire* also provides 34 "recaps" that are not retained. These are curious news summaries provided by the *Business News Wire* that don't have any readily identifiable relationship to private placements. The 259 remaining observations include 54 foreign firms, that are also dropped.

These 205 observations are reduced to 147 observations after excluding firms with no discoverable returns data on the CRSP tapes. Banks and other financial institutions are excluded from this study, as available slack measures are complicated given the inordinately liquid mix of a bank's assets. This reduces the sample by an additional seven firms. Of the 140 remaining firms, thirteen are dropped due to unavailable inside ownership data on *Compaq Disclosure*. These 127 firms are reduced by nine due to unavailable CRSP data for the primary event period. An additional three firms are dropped because both the number of shares issued and the dollar size of the announced private placements are not known.

Of the remaining firms, some announce only the dollar size of the private placement or the number of shares issued. For these, an average discount of fully reporting firms is adopted based on the partially reporting firm's share price five days before the announcement. In other words, where an issue price is available either thorough imputation or in the announcement itself and either the dollar size or number of shares issued is available, the missing variable (number of shares issued or dollars received in the placement) can be easily deducted. Where both the number of shares issued and the dollar size is not given in the announcement, this procedure cannot be accomplished.

Each of the 115 announcements is scrutinized. Detailed examination illustrates that 16 of the firms do not fulfill the data requirements of this study. The observations are dropped for a variety of reasons. These include:

1. The private placement announcement (ppa) is of a private convertible conversion into common.
2. The ppa is of an earlier tender offer to buy by members of the founding family.
3. The ppa is of a purchase, not a sale.
4. The ppa relates the sale to a merger stock purchase agreement.
5. The ppa is made simultaneously with announcements of significant debt issues, public common stock issues, merger and acquisition activities or primary Nasdaq registration fulfillments.

6. The ppa does not provide a convincing event date, with referance to other and unlocateable public announcements of the private placement.

After this 16 firm reduction, the sample is left with 99 observations. Three more firms are lost because the first available ownership data is provided more than one year after the announcement. After a check of the *Wall Street Journal* Index, another firm is lost due to an announcement during the primary event window of a senior convertible note issue. Eight-six firms remain in the sample announcing 95 private placements.

Nine of these firms have sufficient data on the Research Annual File of *Compustat*. Fifty-nine are available on the Full Coverage Annual File of *Compustat*. There is one firm repeated on both tapes. Twenty firms are dropped due to unavailable *Compustat* data on either file. One firm has sufficient data for one of its issues, but not the other. Sixty-seven firms announcing 75 placements remain.

In a final cleansing of the data set, six announcements by five firms are dropped. Two of these are lost due to simultaneous stock sales by management; given the information asymmetry resolution cloud cast on market responses to the private placement announcement by these two firms, they are excluded. One firm is lost due to a simultaneous dividend change. One placement is merely a private sale between shareholders with no liquidity accruing to the firm, so it is also dropped. Two final observations are excluded as one is a second announcement of an earlier included issue and the other is dropped due to a simultaneous significant financing announcement.[88] The ultimate data set thus includes 69 announcements by 62 firms of independent private placements of equity.

The text of the private placement announcements generally discloses the relative and absolute size of the placements, private investor characteristics, proposed uses of the private placement proceeds, perceived needs by firms in the sample for slack, information on the ownership structure changes resulting from the private placements and whether the issue is registered (i.e. unrestricted). Characteristics of the placements, the firms making the placements, the purchasers of the placements and the placement purposes are given in Chapter Four.

3.9 Tests for Model Misspecification and Violations of the Assumptions Underlying the Classical Linear Regression Model

Given that the laboratory used in these examinations is not perfect, a number of statistical "maladies" deserve redress. Although the event-study methodologies adopted by this study are conventional, limitations of the methodology and the data employed deserve mention before the results are provided in Chapter Four. Several econometric problems arise.

3.9.1 Normality of Returns and Calculation of Test Statistics

Assuming the returns from the private placement announcing firms are normally distributed[89], a t-statistic is constructed to illustrate the significance or non-significance of the firms' returns at the time of the announcement. The value of the test statistic is calculated in the traditional fashion to determine the meaningfulness of the observed adjusted abnormal returns.

3.9.2 Influential Outliers

Influential outliers are observations that significantly impact parameter estimates for an entire data set. With larger samples, this impact is generally reduced. (Outliers are often the result of measurement or data entry error.) Several methods for detecting outliers and measuring their impact are considered. Inasmuch as the final sample is less than 70 observations, a moderate level of concern exists for the potential compromise of this study's results by one or more outliers.

The R-Student is a measure of an observation's residual divided by the standard error of a data set excluding the observation. R-student values are provided for each observation to insure that no one individual data point or small sub-sample drives this study's results. Among other diagnostics for misspecification used to measure the influence of outliers is the DFFITS (an acronym for the difference in the "fit" of an examined model) measure; it measures the change in the predicted value when an observation is included to estimate parameters. DFBETAs (an acronym for the difference in the beta estimate of an examined model) are measures of changes in coefficient estimates when a potentially influential observation is included. As with DFFITS, these changes are scaled by the standard error and provide a statistic that measures the change in an estimate relative to the standard error. Changes greater than 3 or 4 times the standard error deserve additional scrutiny.

3.9.3 Multicollinearity and the Use of Dummy Variables

In a collinear environment, the OLS procedure may not be given enough independent variation to calculate effects on random variables. OLS estimation in the presence of multicollinearity is unbiased and still BLUE. Its primary effect is one of causing large variance of the estimates. It is inefficient compared to a model uncompromised by multicollinearity. Given an expectation of multicollinearity between the explanatory variables, a correlation matrix is provided for all variables and variance inflation factors (VIF) are calculated. An acceptable case is where the VIF < 10 or the correlation of an examined regressor with other regressors is less than .9.

$$\text{where } VIF_{RegressorA} = \frac{1}{1 - \text{correlation "} A \text{" with other regressors}}$$

The model may be compromised by multicollinearity and some efficiency may be sacrificed.[90] Any multicollinearity between the independent variables reduces the absolute value of the measure of significance of those variables.

3.9.4 Heteroskedasticity

Another assumption of CLR is that the disturbances are spherical; the data have uniform variance and the error terms are uncorrelated. If the variance is not uniform, the disturbances are said to be heteroskedastic. The parameter estimates are unbiased, but valid inferences based on statistics using measures of the variance are precluded.

The estimating relationships used in this study are likely to be characterized by heteroskedastic disturbances. Among the remedies available to generate efficient estimators that are robust to heteroskedasticity are White standard errors. These weight the OLS parameter estimates of the model by the square root of the relevant diagonal element of the "consistent covariance of estimates" matrix.[91] A heteroskedasticity-corrected t-value results.[92] These are provided later for the examined variables.

3.9.5 Sample Selection Bias

Reference to Appendix 1 provides several insights into the potential for this study's compromise by sample selection bias. If, for example, firms are provided the license to announce only "good" private placements - since the private placements are, by definition, exempt from the registration requirements of a public equity offering to investors - then it could be that the observed positive abnormal returns are nothing more than a favorable bias imposed on the markets by management in their selective announcements.

At least 3 other selection biases have been described: (1) There may be a small-firm bias as large firms are excluded from the sample as they announce "competing" events vs. the lack of coverage of smaller firms; (2) a large-firm bias may develop as small firms are excluded due to a lack of needed CRSP, *Compustat* or *Compaq Disclosure* data; (3) a parameter estimation bias arises as firms become more or less risky after the private placement announcement. Parameter estimates generated before and after the announcement and a separate examination of excluded large firms determine whether the first and last biases impact this study's results. A separate examination of excluded small firms is impractical.

3.10 Concluding Econometric Remarks

A useful model is not one that is necessarily perfect; it is one that is plausible and informative. Given the theory developed above and the empirics examined in the succeeding pages, an optimal liquidity hypothesis and its predictions have intuitive appeal. Economic theory, then, implies a defense of this model. However, the model's vulnerability to sample selection bias, the extensive use of proxies in these theoretical examinations, the presence of many needed and non-separating hypothesis variables, and the potential non-linearity of several of the estimating relationships are statistical issues that temper the results provided in the next chapter.

3.11 NOTES

65. A simplifying assumption is adopted in Figure 1 that allows for a symmetry in the functions plotting the locus of the expected costs of financial slack and free cash flow. This symmetry is not an empirical prediction of the optimal liquidity hypothesis.

66. A similar specification can be derived where the change in stock price is expressed as a quadratic function of an intercept term, a single-powered liquidity variable and a squared liquidity factor.

67. The need for liquidity for a growing firm is represented - as in Figure 2 - by a shift upward and to the right in the benefits of additional liquidity in Figure 2b; this in turn results in a shift to the right in the optimal level of liquidity. A new optimum is indicated at L**. In a similar vein and as illustrated by Figure 3, the firm with an entrenched management and fewer "tolerable" needs for slack is illustrated by a shift upward and to the left in the function illustrating the expected marginal costs of free cash flow in Figure 3b. A shift to the left in the liquidity optimum is represented by L***.

68. ReferencingTable 1 and the 1994 User's Guide of *Compustat,* this is the ratio of shares sold in the placement as stated in the announcement - or as stated in the proxy statement if the announcement is unclear as to the number of shares - divided by the sum of the shares sold in the placement plus the most recent Annual Data Item Number 25 from page 5–40 of the User's Guide. This data item is the Common Shares Outstanding at year-end for the annual file. This number excludes treasury shares and scrip.

69. A negative "discount" represents a premium paid by the purchaser.

70. No set "event window" is favored by all researchers. In the interest of consistency and building on prior studies of private placements, the four-day window starting three days before the private placement announcement is used.

71. A test is later conducted to account for potential pre- and post-parameter estimation bias. There may be a change in the variability of a stock's returns after the placement announcement. Pre-event parameter estimates are biased and misspecified if the return variability change modifies the covariance of the stock's return with the market. To account for this, a second set of parameter estimates are prepared over the period from day 11 to day 151. If the results using these two parameter estimation paradigms are similar, then the results are robust to this estimation bias.

72. A technique for estimating switching regressions is suggested for later research. See Goldfeld and Quandt's (1976) discourse upon "tech-

niques for estimating switching regressions" in *Studies in Nonlinear Estimation.* Kane and Unal (1990) extend Goldfeld and Quandt (1976) and develop a model that assists in the discovery of turning points in the adjusted abnormal returns function, if they exist. Parameter estimation proceeds in a number of steps encouraged by Kane and Unal (1990). The methodologies described by Goldfeld and Quandt (1976) and extended by Kane and Unal (1990) can be used to specify the sign and location of any structural shifts.

73.   A second way to motivate an empirical relationship is to assume that firms are forever optimizing their selected levels of liquidity. These optimal levels of liquidity vary across firms and industries. The only manner with which a representative firm value function can be traced is through the use of size and industry-based normalized measures of liquidity. Factors are employed in this study to control for these variations.

74.   Pilotte (1992) describes tempered negative seasoned equity issue announcement period returns in the framework of several growth proxies. He proposes that firms with growth options encounter a more willing stock market as they issue stock than will firms without these prospects. He provides indirect support for an optimal liquidity hypothesis and encourages this variable as a proxy for slack needs.

75.   A financial distress variable adopted below controls for a money-losing firm in a mature industry that also has a low earnings/price measure. For example, if a U.S. steelmaker is losing money, its deceptively low earnings/price measure implies possession of growth options. The financial distress variable controls for this empirical issue.

76.   A naive student investigating market responses to a company's announcement of new external financing might expect a favorable stockholder impact. The money raising activity "should" signal favorable investment opportunities and the ability of the firm to add to shareholder value. An empirical prediction evolves that announcements of external financing should lead to increases in market value.

77.   Alternatively, the cash-flow-signaling hypothesis supported by Miller and Rock (1985) implies an unfavorable reception by the market of news that firm activities are generating lower cash flows than previously revealed. However, this "news" and its impact on stock price is captured by the size and discount of the placement, as the purchaser discloses this asymmetry in his or her purchase terms.

78.   Jensen and Meckling (1976) consider the benefits of increased management ownership and Shleifer and Vishny (1986), the benefits of large shareholders.

79.   This is not the methodology used by Wruck (1989). She employs a measure of the change in ownership concentration in her study.

80.   Johnson, Serrano and Thompson (1996), in a similar vein, examine the stockholder wealth effects of insider sales around the announcement of equity issues. Their findings actually support an information hypothesis - considered in the next section. They present evidence that management buying just before equity issue announcements significantly reduces the negative market responses generally observed at equity issue announcements.

81.   The "management sells" signal provides a favorable ownership structure impact, however, where management ownership is presumed to be better aligned with shareholders following the sale. This variable may be positive where the ownership moves from the less desirable middle level of ownership to one of the more favored "tails" of less than 5% or over 25% ownership concentration. The signs of both a management buyer and management seller factor are subject to a simultaneous asymmetric release of information not captured by one of the other variables in the model.

82.   A "foreign investor" variable is encouraged by Hertzel and Smith (1993) and may capture ownership structure effects. Additionally, if the foreign or single investor overpaid for the private placement, a hubris hypothesis may have explanatory power. There may be no price effects or negative effects if there have been prior information releases or if the investor overpaid.

83.   Examinations by Lummer and McConnell (1989), James (1987) and Gilson, John and Lang (1990) shed light on the importance of debt to monitor management.

84.   This segues with Frankel, McNichols and Wilson (1995), who observe fewer information asymmetries and more news releases for the firms most actively engaged in financing activity.

85.   SIC codes are used in an attempt to measure performance relative to a firm's industry. However, the use of SIC codes to generate industry-normalized measures as benchmarks proves impractical.

86.   The power of restricted shares variables may be reduced, however, since studies by Wruck (1989) and Hertzel and Smith (1993). Barron (1995) outlines options available to restricted shareholders to sell their securities under new SEC guidelines. Appendix 1 provides a review of these recent policy changes.

87.   Some cross-sectional analyses may be compromised by the expected absence of small-firm data. The smallest firm may be in the greatest need of

slack and dropping these observations diminishes results supporting the optimal liquidity hypothesis.

88. Ambarish, John and Williams (1987) and Loderer and Mauer (1992) consider the information effects of simultaneous signals of investment, dividends and equity issues; they suggest equity issues and the private placement story are clouded where issuing firms make simultaneous announcements of these other activities.

89. A Bera-Jaque default test for normality is available in SAS and other tests for normality include a Kolomogorov-Smirnov test and various sign tests.

90. Another rule-of-thumb is not to worry about multicollinearity if the $|t| > 2$ for H_0: Parameter Value = 0.

91. The use of White standard errors assumes that no other "problems" than heteroskedasticity exist with the data; this examination assumes away problems such as simultaneity. White adjusts only for heteroskedasticity.

92. Another technique used to generate a heteroskedasticity-consistent variance/covariance matrix and estimators robust to heteroskedasticity is the method of weighted least squares (WLS). This approach weights a model by some component that produces homoskedasticity, or a tolerable - by specification standards - level of heteroskedasticity. The dependent and independent variables can, for example, be divided by the residual standard error for the market model estimation period.

CHAPTER 4

Optimal Liquidity Levels and Private Equity Placements

4.1 Outline and Objectives of Chapter Four

The primary objective of the study is to examine the evidence concerning the premise that slack creation can be wealth-enhancing. Earlier studies provide the theoretical basis for this examination. The authors of those studies propose that there is a relationship between firm value and firm liquidity levels. Based upon the theory, there should be a relationship between firm value and returns observed at announcements of private placements of equity that is based, at least in part, on liquidity effects. This chapter provides an empirical examination and cross-sectional study of the relationship between liquidity and firm value effects arising during private placement announcements.

Chapter four is organized as follows: the sample is described and summary data are provided and contrasted to earlier studies of private placements in the next section; unadjusted and adjusted announcement period returns are given in Section 4.3; empirical predictions and tests of an optimal liquidity hypothesis are outlined in Section 4.4; limitations of the results in Section 4.4 are described in Section 4.5; the final section reviews the research questions and concludes the empirical examinations.

4.2 Sample Description and Summary Data

The 69 separate private placement announcements by 62 firms between 1988 and 1995 are described in Tables 2-6A.[93] The text of the
private placement announcements varies. Several of the announcements are exhaustive and provide extensive data on the relative and
absolute size of the placements, private investor characteristics, proposed use of the private placements proceeds, perceived needs by
the firms for the arriving liquidity, information on the ownership
structure changes resulting from the private placement and whether
the issues are registered or unregistered (i.e. restricted). A few of the
announcements, however, are brief. The announcements vary in
size from 60 words to several hundred.

Referencing Table 2, the mean size of the placements is less
than $5 million; this small placement size is further highlighted by
a median placement size of only $2.2 million. The largest place-
ment is for $22.5 million. The fraction placed in the private issues
varies from less than 1% to 39.5% of shares outstanding after the
placement. Using outstanding shares as reported in *Compaq Disclosure,* the average and median fractions placed are around 10%,
with the median slightly less than the mean. Discounts given to the
private placement purchasers by the issuing firms vary, as well.
The greatest discount relative to the firm's publicly traded stock
price 5 days before the announcement is 78.6%. The smallest "discount" is a premium paid of 50% over the firm's stock price. The
mean and median discounts are just over 20%. Sixteen of the issues
are of registered shares, 24 of unregistered shares and 29 of the
announcements do not disclose the registered (unrestricted) or
unregistered (restricted) status of the issue. The issuing activity is
concentrated in the last 3 years of the sample period.

Characteristics of the firms making the placement announcements are given in Table 3. Firms have most recent, relative to the
announcement, annually reported asset sizes in *Compustat* ranging
from around $1/2 million to over $70 million. Market values of
equity based on share prices 5 days before the issue and most recent
annually reported shares outstanding range from $3.3 million to
just less than $1/2 billion. Mean and median asset sizes of $17.5 million and $10.6 million, respectively, are reported. Inside ownership
before the private issues vary from less than 2% to over 82% for the
issuing firms. The mean and median inside ownership levels are

both around a quarter with the median slightly less than the mean. Book-to-market equity ratios range from around 0 for one firm with marginally negative reported stockholders equity to a maximum of 1.65. This measure is developed using market prices 5 days before the issue and the most recent annually reported stockholders equity in *Compustat*. A mean book-to-market equity ratio of .294 is observed, with a median of .177. As with the asset size and issue size measures, averages are pushed upwards by the larger observation measures, with meaningful illustrations of the distributions of the sample given by the medians. Forty-three of the announcements are preceded by two prior years of negative earnings and are presumed to be in a relative degree of financial distress.

Table 4 gives characteristics of the purchasers of the private placements in the sample of 69 issues. All of the purchaser information is taken from the text of the private placement announcements in the *Business News Wire*. No single group dominates the purchaser descriptions. Sixteen of the purchasers are single and/or foreign. Twenty-four are institutional or corporate with all of the corporate buyers in related businesses. Nine of the purchasers are managers or directors at the time of the purchase with 11 outside buyers becoming managers or directors with the purchase. No information on the buyer(s) is given in 26 of the announcements. These characteristics sum to over 69 as many buyers share multiple features.

The purposes of the private placement proceeds are illustrated by Table 5. Purposes are drawn from the text of the announcements. Half (34) of the 69 issues are for new products and 8 are for debt retirement. Twenty-three of the placements generate funds for working capital. Three provide funds to be used, at least partially, in acquisitions. Fourteen of the announcements do not reveal the purpose of the private placement proceeds. The announced funds uses sum to over 69 as many firms report multiple intended uses for their private placement proceeds.

The sample is contrasted in Table 6-A to those used in earlier studies of equity private placements. Contrasting data are drawn from Wruck (1989), Hertzel and Smith (1993), and Tables 2-5 of this study. Purchasers in the three studies are contrasted in Panel A of Table 6-A. The purchaser make-up of this study does not seem to differ greatly from earlier studies. Although the purchaser "mix" is different, no striking dissimilarities based on the manager/director, institutional or individual status of the buyer is noted; the Hertzel and Smith study, however, seems to be dominated relatively by individual and institutional buyers.

Panel B of Table 6-A reveals noteworthy contrasts between this study and others of private placements based on the placement characteristics. The size of the placements used in this study are much smaller than either those of Wruck (1989) or Hertzel and Smith (1993). The average proceeds of the earlier samples are between 30 and 40 million dollars versus the average in this study of less than $5 million. Average discounts granted here are similar to the 20.1% discount in the Hertzel and Smith study, but are far greater than the average discount of less than 5% implied by Wruck.[94] The average fraction placed in the current study of around 12% is less than the average relative portion of stock issued in the previous private placement samples. Wruck's sample averages almost 20% of shares outstanding after the placement and Hertzel and Smith's measures over 16%.

The firm characteristics provided in Panel C of Table 6-A also highlight differences between this sample and those of the earlier works. The firms in this study are much smaller; they average market values of equity of only $66.32 million versus the average capitalizations of $233.7 million in Wruck's (1989) examination and $441.5 million in Hertzel and Smith's (1993) work. The ownership concentrations of the firms in the three studies are similar, however, averaging between 25% and 31% of shares outstanding before the private placement announcements.

The implications of the differences and similarities between this study's sample and earlier works on private placements are not certain. Panel A reveals the institutional and individual make-up of the Hertzel and Smith (1993) study; a greater relative portion of this study's buyers are made up of managers and directors. Depending on the ownership structures prior to the placement, a more favorable response is expected for the Hertzel and Smith sample, with a significant portion of the owner-ship being assumed by new outside blockholders. The ownership mix of this study relative to Wruck's (1989) examination of primarily larger exchange-listed firms does not lead to an expectation of differing market responses to the announcements. The buyers in her study are similar, based on insider and institutional and individual mix, to the ones in the sample of 69 announcements. The small firms in this study's sample may reduce the ownership impact, independent of any similarity in buyer make-up to the Wruck study.

Panels B and C highlight contrasts between this and the earlier private placement samples. It is possible that these are less scrutinized firms followed by fewer analysts and that the market's overall responses will be more extreme than for the larger firms for whom the announcement is less "newsworthy." Conversely, the smaller relative size of the placements illustrated in Panel B leads to an expectation of a smaller market response.

The average fractions placed and discounts given to the purchasers implies a different set of beliefs in the issuing firms by the purchasers in the Wruck (1989) study than in this work. The smaller discount suggests the placements in her study are being made by firms in better financial health than those in this study or whose stock prices prior to announcement better reflect adverse circumstances, if such circumstances exist.

The marginally lower concentrations of ownership prior to the placements revealed in Panel C may suggest a different set of market responses, as well. Insider control of a majority of outstanding common stock develops in many of the earlier studies' firms as a result of the placements. A lower relative portion of the firms in this study develop a similar new majority. If the new majority better "forces" an alignment with shareholder interests or positions the firm for takeover, the response is favorable. It is possible, however, that no significant effect can be attributed to ownership structure. As Morck, Schleifer and Vishny (1988) note, ownership effects are less important with information releases by smaller firms; these ownership effects are more significant for the more closely monitored and larger firms. Thereby, the smaller size of the companies in the current tests, compared to Wruck (1989) and Hertzel and Smith (1993), may mitigate an ownership effect.

4.3 Unadjusted and Adjusted Announcement Period Returns

Logged announcement period abnormal returns are given in Table 7. Panel A includes the traditional and unadjusted mean cumulative abnormal returns (CARs) over the primary event window from 3 days before to the day of the announcement. Panel B provides the mean CARs derived using the adjustment encouraged by Wruck (1989) in Equation 9 from Section 3.2. Primary event window results are supplemented by the reporting of mean CARs over event periods also used by Wruck.

With the exception of two secondary event windows for unadjusted CARs just before and after the firm's private placement announcement, every selected event window exhibits significant abnormal returns. Primary event window average un - adjusted abnormal returns equal .49% and average adjusted abnormal returns equal 2.5%; p-values are less than .04 and .01, respectively.

The impact of the adjustment is greatest for the longest event windows illustrated in Table 7 before, including and after the announcement. For example, the 90 day window from 59 days before to 30 days after the announcement exhibits an unadjusted and significant negative mean cumulative abnormal return of over 16%. However, after adjustments allowing for the size and discounted price of the placement, this unadjusted negative response is rendered significantly positive. This brings the suitability of the adjusted measure for longer windows into question. However, its use by prior authors and applicability for the shorter primary event window seem justified.

The adjustment, as developed in Equation 10 in Chapter 3, is intuitively appealing. If the firm privately issues a significant portion of firm equity, averaging around 12% in this study, at a discount and the market does not penalize stock price, then an effective favorable response is implied even if the stock price change is neutral or moderately negative. The contrast between the positive observed returns in this study and the average negative market reaction to seasoned equity issues, where no discount is intended by management, is very telling even before the adjustments of Equation Ten.

With and without adjustment, the average firms in the sample precede the private placement announcements with significant negative abnormal returns. Beginning 9 days before the event, stock prices reverse this pattern with or without adjustment. The positive abnormal returns are concentrated in the primary event window. P-values in Panels A and B are greater than 5% only for unadjusted event windows 10 days before and after the primary event. The unadjusted period (−9,0) exhibits an abnormal return of .6% with a p-value of 11% and the unadjusted abnormal returns for the period (1,10) are effectively zero. P-values approach 0 for all of the adjusted CARs over every selected event window. The probable sources of the adjusted abnormal returns in the primary event window are examined in the following sections.

4.4 Empirical Predictions and Tests of an Optimal Liquidity Hypothesis

Ordinary least squares regression analysis is used to determine whether or not an optimal liquidity hypothesis is consistent with the "typical" stock price response to new private equity financing announcements. Coefficient signs and significance levels are compared to the predictions. A summary of these predictions for the selected independent variables is provided in Table 8-A. The results of tests in a series of estimating environments are provided in Tables 8-B through 8-H. A final regression allowing for *changes* in ownership concentration is provided in Table 8-I. The model in Table 8-B is drawn directly from Equation 11. Results from Tables 8-C through 8-H omit specific allowances for managerial discretion or ownership structure or the influence of two significant outliers. Results in Table 8-D illustrate the impact of an omission of firm size on the studys result's. Parameter estimates and significance levels in Table 8-E form the foundation of most of this studys conclusions. Tables 8-F through 8-H portray results of tests of ancillary models further supporting the findings of earlier tests.

4.4.1 Proxies for Growth Options in Tests of an Optimal Liquidity Hypothesis

The empirical implications of growth options in tests of an optimal liquidity hypothesis are outlined in Panels A of Tables 8-B through 8-H. The predictions from Equation 11, parameter estimates and P-values for the variables proxying for the strength of this hypothesis are given.

4.4.1.1 Earnings/Price

Consistent with all predictions, the parameter estimate of the "earnings/price" factor for growth options and additional relative needs for liquidity is negative and significant. It is a very robust factor. In multiple tests for sensitivity, its explanatory power is not significantly changed. Successive exclusions of ownership variables, influential outliers and a proxy for firm size in Tables 8-B through 8-H do not significantly reduce the power (maximum p-value = .013) of this factor. Results are uniformly consistent with an optimal liquidity hypothesis; earlier studies (see Pilotte, 1992) find also a positive correlation between equity-issue announcements and a firm's possession of growth options. This positive correlation exists for the current sample with the use of an "inverted" growth factor such as the earnings/price measure employed.

It is not certain that a low earnings/price measure is necessarily an appropriate proxy for growth options (or, for that matter, liquidity needs). A consensus exists in the finance community, however, that where the markets bid up a firm's stock relative to current earnings, a rational expectation must exist that future earnings will increase; the prospect of firm growth is implied.[95]

A separate univariate analysis of firms possessing earnings / price measures above and below the sample median is conducted. The positive returns of the overall sample are not as significant for the firms possessing earnings/price measures above the sample median. Twice as many firms above the sample median experience negative market responses to the announcements as do firms below the median. The firms with higher earnings/price measures are typically larger (though not significantly) and significantly less likely to have had two succeeding prior years of negative earnings.

4.4.1.2 New Product

The sign of the "new product" dummy variable is consistent with an optimal liquidity hypothesis in Table 8-B, but it is not significant. Moreover, the parameter estimate changes signs over successive iterations. Almost half of the firms in the sample (see Table 5) announce private placement funds uses which express or imply a new product investment, but the cross-section of positive abnormal returns is incompletely described by this dummy variable.

4.4.1.3 Working Capital

The final measure of growth options is represented by the "working capital" proxy. In the initial estimation of this factor, firms announcing private equity placements along with an intention to use the placement proceeds to fund working capital are associated with positive market responses. This association is underscored when the less meaningful ownership variables are excluded. Caution needs to be taken, however, with this variable, as the exclusion of later discovered influential observations reveals that much or this factor's power in the entire initial sample derives from a single and influential observation. Care needs to be taken in attaching significance to any variable which depends upon model selection to develop meaning. In successive tests, this factor exhibits changing signs of the coefficient estimate and significant variations in its levels of significance.

4.4.2 *Proxies for Ownership Structure in Tests of an Optimal Liquidity Hypothesis*

Earlier studies of equity issues provide evidence consistent with a reduced role for ownership structure and an increased role of information releases in describing the cross-section of returns for smaller firms making an equity issue.[96] Although the initial inclusion of factors portraying the power of an ownership structure hypothesis is appropriate, as developed in Chapters 2 and 3 above, the small firm sizes and initial results invite the exclusion of these factors in better specified and simpler models succeeding the one in Table 8-B. None of the ownership proxies first adopted are significant in explaining any of this study's results. Separate tests employing a single ownership concentration factor are similarly not noteworthy. Absent the inclusion of ownership factors, explanatory powers of the other most significant factors remain.

In a final test in Table 8-I of factors specifically developed by Wruck (1989), however, evidence is portrayed supporting her and Morck, Schleifer and Vishny (1988). Positive-signed factors for the change in ownership concentration from 0 to 5% and above 25% are revealed. A negative-signed and significant factor is estimated for the entrenched level of inside ownership from 5 to 25%. Tests portrayed in Table 8-I are developed in Section 4.5.

4.4.3 *Proxies for Liquidity in Tests of an Optimal Liquidity Hypothesis*

The empirical implications of direct measures of liquidity in tests of an optimal liquidity hypothesis are outlined in Panels C of Tables 8-B through 8-H. Two direct measures of liquidity and changes in liquidity and two interactive liquidity measures are employed in tests of an optimal liquidity hypothesis.

4.4.3.1 Liquidity

Markets appear to condition their responses to private placement announcements based upon a firm's "liquidity." Median liquidity levels before the announcements equal 43.1% of the preceding fully reported year's liquidity needs. In an unreported test excluding a factor for the change in liquidity, these existing liquidity levels are positively and significantly related (p-value = .032) to market responses to the announcements. This result is not consistent with predictions of an optimal liquidity hypothesis, but has some appeal if the markets condition a firm's prospects based upon its available liquid resources. The liquidity measure is not robust, however, to the inclusion of a factor for the change in liquidity levels.[97]

None of the results illustrated in Tables 8-B through 8-H attach any significance to liquidity if the change in liquidity is also a factor. The greatest changes in liquidity, not surprisingly, occur for the firms with the initially lowest levels of liquidity. The liquidity variable is omitted from two of the last three cross-sectional iterations in Tables 8-F and 8-H. This omission affirms the robustness of other factors examined below.

4.4.3.2 Change in Liquidity

Consistent with an optimal liquidity hypothesis for firms well to the left of their optima in Figure 1, the change-in-liquidity factor is positive and significant in describing market responses. Of all measures of liquidity examined in this study, the simple arithmetic change in liquidity is the most significant and robust in describing market responses. The "change in liquidity" variable is sensitive to the leverage of the two most influential observations in the initial sample of 69 announcements. The inclusion of ownership structure variables and influential observations in Tables 8-B and 8-C disguises the significance of the liquidity changes. P-values of less than .034 for this variable are reported in all other models. The change in liquidity factor is the most significant variable in the modeling encouraged by Wruck (1989) in Table 8-I, when changes in ownership concentration are considered.

A separate univariate analysis of firms based upon their reported changes in liquidity is conducted. Average changes in liquidity equal 29.4% of the preceding year's liquidity needs. The smallest firms are significantly related to the largest changes in liquidity. New product announcements are associated with the greatest changes in liquidity, as well. Firms in financial distress are also very likely to be receiving the largest infusions of liquidity relative to their annual operating needs. Firms that receive a change in liquidity above the sample median are associated with an average market response three times as positive as those below the median. The greatest liquidity changes occur for the firms initially possessing the lowest levels of liquidity.

4.4.3.3 Product of Liquidity and Change in Liquidity

This interactive variable is suggested in the derivation of Equations 8 and 11 and is portrayed in Equation 7. It is not employed in Equation 11, but is examined separately. An optimal liquidity hypothesis suggesting a negative-signed liquidity variable and a positive-signed change in liquidity factor predicts a negative and significant parameter estimate for this variable. However, the factor is positive and significant (p-value = .015) in a set of ancillary tests when initial and changing liquidity levels are ignored. It is not robust to the inclusion of any other liquidity factor. Other parameter estimates are not significantly changed when this factor is employed alone as a liquidity proxy or in tandem with other liquidity measures. This factor is not robust and no overall significance can be attached to this variable.

4.4.3.4 Liquidity Squared

This factor is employed to test, in the simplest manner, for the existence of a liquidity optimum. No significance can be attributed to this variable. Similar to the interactive liquidity measure above, no significance attaches to this factor when other liquidity measures are included. A p-value of .117 results and the coefficient estimate is positive, contrary to the suggestions of an optimal liquidity hypothesis, when it is included as the only "direct" liquidity measure in a set of unreported tests. This limited significance disappears when a change in liquidity variable is included.

4.4.4 *Control Variables in Tests of an Optimal Liquidity Hypothesis*

The empirical implications of a set of control variables in tests of an optimal liquidity hypothesis are outlined in Panels D of Tables 8-B through 8-H. A set of factors used in earlier private placement studies is adopted to control for information releases related to firm size, performance and the nature of the securities being privately issued.

4.4.4.1 *Financial Distress*[98]

One of these control variables is the "financial distress" factor. This factor is insignificant and no power can be attributed to it. It is neither an efficient nor a robust variable. Its only noteworthy impact is that it moderately depresses the power of the change-in- liquidity variable in describing market responses (see Tables 8-E and 8-F). This factor's limited significance is echoed in all of this study's tests. It is dropped in the final modelings of Tables 8-F through 8-H.

4.4.4.2 *Restricted Shares*

Earlier studies of private placement announcements attach positive significance to a dummy for privately issued but "restricted shares." The least liquid firms are much more likely to issue restricted, than unrestricted, shares. Unregistered shares are also more likely to be issued by the smallest firms in the sample.

With the purchase of an unsaleable equity interest, a buyer provides a costly signal of firm value based on the size and discount afforded to his or her purchase. However, referring to the comments in Appendix 1, a reduced significance for this variable is expected. Securities laws now provide a greater ease of selling "unsaleable" shares versus the time of the last widely published study of market responses to private placement announcements. This expectation is borne out as this factor achieves no significance in the "best" model of Table 8-F (p-value = .128). It is insignificant in all other tests.

4.4.4.3 *Prior Underperformance*

A third control variable is one for "prior underperformance." The underperforming firm is expected to benefit from the announcement of a private placement. However, prior underperformance is ultimately modeled as a precursor to adverse market responses. The underperforming firm is less likely than its counterparts to announce a new product or working capital investment. The average negative market responses to the underperforming firm implies that performance similar to the market's is a proxy for the survivability of the firm.

Prior underperformance may proxy for the likelihood of a firm's failure. Investors condition their responses based upon their belief in the longevity of the firm. This belief can be manifested, in part, by negative responses to the firm which has recently underperformed the market or which is slack-poor. In tests of the appropriateness of an underperformance proxy in describing abnormal returns, this factor is negative and significant, with p-values between .092 (Table 8-D) and .068 (Table 8-E). It is less significant than the factors "firm size", "change in liquidity" and "earnings/price" in all reported and unreported tests.

4.4.4.4 Firm Size

The final variable selected to describe market responses to these announcements is one for firm size. Using the log of firm size based upon total assets, a negative and significant sign is predicted for this factor. "Firm size" is negative and significant and is discovered later to be robust to a number of statistical issues confronting the data in this study. With and without the inclusion of variables proxying for an ownership structure hypothesis and after exclusion of influential outliers, firm size is a robust variable describing market responses in a number of estimating environments. It is negative and significant in the final selected model. The negative significance of this firm size variable in describing the cross-section of stock returns is consistent with earlier studies.

The largest firms are associated with both the smallest initial liquidity levels and with the smallest changes in liquidity. Size may be inversely related to the need for liquidity. The larger and better known firm may have similar needs for liquidity relative to its smaller counterpart. However, the larger firm may have more immediate access to "risk-free" and unreported borrowing rights than its smaller brethren. In effect, the larger firm has higher, yet unreported available liquidity, if this borrowing access is included. This may explain an element of the inverse and significant relationship between firm size and market responses, where markets discourage the greater liquidity accumulation by larger firms which, by their size, already have greater relative access to liquidity.

As a test to determine whether or not "firm size" is displacing direct liquidity proxies in explaining returns, it is excluded from a test in Table 8-D. The power of the change in liquidity factor is markedly increased (p-value less than .001 in Table 8-D). The change in significance is consistent with firm size displacing the size of the liquidity change in describing market responses. No other significant effects are evident after a cursory review of the impact on coefficient estimates of a dropping of the firm size variable. Results are consistent with firm size proxying for available liquidity, as the larger firm is presumed to have greater and more immediate access to liquidity through its average longer term lending relationships and typically greater market exposure.

4.5 Tests of Hertzel and Smith (1993) and Wruck (1989)

A final set of tests are conducted to examine the power of the specific factors adopted to explain market responses in prior private placement studies. These tests measure the relative significance of this study's results in explaining market responses.

4.5.1 Hertzel and Smith (1993)

Many of the factors employed in this study are constructed using traditional event-study methodologies used earlier by Hertzel and Smith (1993). These "traditional" factors include the unregistered shares, placement buyer type, new product and financial distress dummy variables. Among the factors not specifically adopted by this study and employed in the Hertzel and Smith (1993) work is an independent variable "fraction placed." Adopted in a set of unreported tests, this variable is directly employed in the construction of the dependent variable in Equation 10. Its meaningfulness in a cross-sectional regression is expected. This linear dependence between left and right-hand-side variables results in a p-value of less than .01 and a reduction in the significance of the earnings/price and change in liquidity factors in that set of tests.

Inasmuch as the fraction placed variable is determined simultaneously with the adjusted abnormal return dependent variable, it is excluded from this study's reported tests.

4.5.2 *Wruck (1989)*

Test results are given in Table 8-I that include a set of ownership change variables developed by Wruck (1989). These results are consistent with her premise, considered earlier by Morck, Schleifer and Vishny (1988), that firm value is a non-monotonic function of levels of inside ownership. Firm value is expected to increase with increasing ownership at lower levels between 0 and 5% of inside ownership, decrease up to 25% inside ownership and increase thereafter. Tests do not reject this expectation, with signs of parameter estimates as expected at all three levels, but are significant only in the middle level of inside ownership. Negative market responses are associated with increasing levels of inside ownership in the entrenched levels of ownership concentration between 5 and 25%.

The inclusion of the ownership structure changes adopted by Wruck (1989) has other effects. The significance of the change in liquidity factor is underscored. It becomes the single most significant factor in the model of Table 8-I. The earnings/price factor loses much of its statistical significance. The negative significance of the new product variable is troublesome and may suggest a free cash flow overinvestment dilemma. Firm size and underperformance factors retain their negative statistical significance.

Overall, the model of Table 8-I is impressive. It underscores the importance of liquidity changes in describing market responses to private placement announcements. The results also highlight the significance of *changes* in ownership concentration for smaller firms; these firms are not expected to have market responses to firm events closely associated with the structure of firm ownership.

4.6 Limitations of the Statistical Results

The proxies adopted and methodologies employed in this study are not perfect, and a number of statistical issues that compromise test results are anticipated. The proxies, sample selection and methodologies are customary, but each invites statistical review as the tests are conducted.

4.6.1 Normality of Returns and Calculations of Test Statistics

A p-value is used to illustrate the significance or non-significance of the firms' returns at the time of the announcement. This p-value and calculated t-values assume a normality of returns distributions. P-values are provided for the primary event window using parameter estimates developed over estimation periods before and after the announcement date. P-values are given using a pre-event estimation period. The potential of post-parameter estimation biases and influential outliers to compromise the normality of returns distributions are considered below.

4.6.2 Influential Outliers

Influential outliers are observations that significantly impact parameter estimates for an entire data set. With any sample of only 69 observations, a moderate level of concern exists for the potential compromise of results by one or more outliers.[99] Two of the 69 announcements of private placements of equity are very influential. Announcements by Sonic Environmental and Versus Technology generate high R-Student values and significant measures of DFFITS and DFBETAs. This is not surprising when the entire vector attaching to each of these two observations is considered. Sonic Environmental grants the largest discount to its buyer of all the discounts granted in the entire sample and the fraction placed is also the highest within the sample. Coupling these together in the adjusted abnormal returns measure of Equation 10, which constructs the dependent variable in this study, causes its influence. An R-Student of over 8 leads to this observation's exclusion. Versus Technology receives the highest premium of all the private placement issuers in this study, thus leading to its influence and exclusion, as well.

4.6.2.1 Sample Description and Summary Data After Influential Outlier Exclusion

Data are given describing the final set of 67 announcements in Table 6-B. These data are contrasted with the 69 announcements meeting the initial requirements for inclusion. Given the reasons for the exclusion of the two influential outliers, the most marked contrasts between this 67 observation set and the earlier one are expected. Purchaser and firm characteristics in Panels A and C of Table 6-B exhibit no significant change. However, the impact of the outlier exclusion on the "maximum fraction placed" and "minimum discount" measures are significant. The "maximum fraction placed" drops from almost 40% to less than 35% and the "minimum discount" (maximum premium) changes to less than −17% from −50%. Summary data for the new set of 67 observations are virtually unchanged, but the impact of the outlier exclusion on the "tails" of the examined sample is noteworthy.

4.6.2.2 Unadjusted and Adjusted Announcement Period Returns After Influential Observation Exclusion

Tests on the impact of these two most influential observations are conducted to measure their influence on overall sample returns. Contrasting Table 9 with Table 7 reveals that the two announcements play a moderate role in influencing overall sample returns. Unadjusted and adjusted cumulative abnormal returns over the longest and primary event windows are provided in Panels A and B of Table 9 after excluding the two most influential observations in the sample. Among the impacts of this exclusion is the reduction in significance of the unadjusted mean cumulative abnormal returns (CARs) over the primary event window. The mean CAR in Panel A of Table 7 is significant at the 5% level for the primary event window (−3, 0) when including Sonic Environmental and Versus Technology. The mean CAR over this same period is not significant after exclusion of those observations. However, excluding the most influential observations does not temper the very high significance of the more closely scrutinized adjusted measure in Panel B of Tables 7 and 9. After exclusion, the adjusted mean CAR over the primary event window is positive and significant. Returns over the longest event window (−59,30) are marginally lower when the two most influential observations are excluded.

4.6.2.3 Cross-sectional Test Results After Influential Observation Exclusion

Results portrayed following Table 8-C, except for a post-parameter estimation in Table 12-A, include only the sample excluding the

two most influential observations. Impacts of these two announcements are evident in a contrast of Tables 8-C and 8-E. The "working capital" factor changes signs and becomes insignificant. All of
its earlier significance derives from a single observation. The
"change in liquidity" variable is insignificant in the initial sample.
Upon outlier exclusion, this factor becomes significant, with p-
values of less than .035 in all succeeding tests. The estimate and
significance of "prior underperformance" is significantly impacted
also by significant outlier inclusion. Whereas earlier in Tables 8-B
and 8-C the factor for underperformance is insignificant, it
becomes negative and significant following Table 8-C with p-
values of less than .10. Significance levels of the factors "firm
size" and "restricted shares" are increased in tests of the smaller
final sample, as well. The "earnings/price" factor maintains its
significance in most estimating environments. The significances
of both change in liquidity and underperformance factors are
found when the two outliers are excluded. A set of misleading
and incomplete conclusions are revealed absent the exclusion of
these two most influential outliers.

4.6.3 Multicollinearity and the Use of Dummy Variables

A primary assumption of the classical linear regression model is
that no exact linear relationship exists between the independent
variables. No exact linear relationship between the explanatory
variables is expected. However, with an expectation of some multicollinearity, a correlation matrix and schedule of variance inflation
factors (VIFs) is examined for all variables. A schedule of the VIFs
is given in Table 10-A. All of these measures for all of the variables
fall within acceptable limits.

Pearson correlation coefficients are given in Table 10-B. Data in
that table reveal a high degree of correlation among the "new product," "working capital," "financial distress," and "liquidity" variables. The correlation is greatest between the variables "liquidity"
and "change in liquidity." The model of Table 8-F is constructed
to examine the importance of these correlations in impacting
parameter estimates and levels of significance. The robustness
and significance of "earnings/price," "change in liquidity," "prior
underperformance," and "firm size" variables are underscored by

the results portrayed in Table 8-F. Multicollinearity does not significantly compromise any of this study's conclusions.

4.6.4 Heteroskedasticity

Heteroskedastic disturbances characterize the estimating relationships in this study. White standard errors are used to generate efficient estimators that are robust to heteroskedasticity. These provide estimates of a heteroskedasticity-corrected t-value for H_0: parameter value = 0. Weighting the OLS parameter estimates of Equation 11 by the square root of the relevant diagonal element of the "consistent covariance of estimates" matrix provides this corrected t-value. Uncorrected t-values and t-values corrected using White standard errors are given for each variable in Tables 11-A and 11-B for models portrayed by Tables 8-E and 8-F. With successive reductions in the number of independent variables employed in this study's analyses, declining p-values from White's specification tests imply greater needs for corrections due to hetreoskedasticity. White's measures are not significant in the models of Tables 8-B and 8-C.

There are no significant reductions in the powers of the test statistics when corrections are made for heteroskedasticity using White's method. In fact, several of the t-values are improved. However, dependance upon increased t-values in Tables 11-A and 11-B after corrections using White's method is ill-advised with a sample of only 67 observations. Significance levels before corrections are not diminished, but conclusions that p-values and significances are increased cannot be reached. All that can be concluded is that the ability of the optimal liquidity hypothesis to describe announcement period abnormal returns is not threatened by non-spherical disturbances.

4.6.5 Sample Selection Biases

Three selection biases are described in this study: (1) A small-firm bias arises as large firms are excluded from the sample as the financial press reports "competing" events; fewer such events are reported for the smaller firms; (2) a large-firm bias may develop as small firms are excluded due to a lack of needed CRSP, *Compustat* or *Compaq Disclosure* data; (3) a parameter estimation bias can arise as firms become more or less risky after the private placement announcement.

Relative to the first bias above, only one firm is excluded from the final sample due to competing announcements elsewhere. Most primary event window "news" for firms later excluded from the final sample is included in the *Business News Wire* announcement. This limits the first bias above. The large firm bias in (2) above is problematical; no practical fashion exists to examine the contrasting behavior of firms excluded due to lack of needed data, as that data is required to generate meaningful portraits of those excluded firm's behavior.

Parameter estimates generated before and after the announcement determine whether the third bias impacts this study's results. Measures of this bias are illustrated in Tables 12-A and 12-B for the full sample of 69 announcements and the abbreviated sample of 67 announcements. Using parameter estimates generated after the announcement date[100], abnormal returns are calculated in the traditional fashion using Equation 9 and adjusted using Equation 10. Unadjusted abnormal returns are given in Panels A of Tables 12-A and 12-B using the post-event estimation period. The adjusted abnormal returns measures using these parameter estimates are given in Panel B. Overall mean CAR values for both samples and in all panels of Tables 12-A and 12-B are tempered using parameters estimated over the period following the private placement announcement.

The post-event estimation of parameters greatly diminishes the significance of the unadjusted abnormal returns measures, from a p-value of .04 to one over .13 for the 69 firms in Panel A of Table 12-A. The adjusted measure for the primary event window remains positive and significant. The exclusion of the influential announcements leads to reductions in the unadjusted abnormal returns measure in Panel A of Table 12-B. The 67 firms exhibit a positive, yet insignificant, abnormal return with a p-value of .21.

The final indicator of the impact of post-parameter estimation bias is in the second panel of Table 12-B. The primary event window, after post-parameter estimation adjustment and with the adjustments of Equation 10, exhibits positive and significant abnormal returns. Given the similar size and significance of the adjusted measure after post-event parameter estimation, this bias does not compromise this study's findings.

4.6.6 *Appropriateness of Selected Proxies for Examined Hypotheses*

The appropriateness of the selected proxies for the underlying theories is a continuing statistical concern in the academic community. Although care is taken to insure a clear link between the selected proxies and their adjacent theories, some overlap across theories by the proxies is expected.

4.7 Conclusions and Review of Research Questions

This study proposes that adverse market responses to the average announcement by publicly traded firms of an intent to issue equity are tempered where a firm has an observable need for liquidity to meet operating needs or pursue profitable investment. All that is required to investigate the strength of this proposal is a liquidity changing event, an observable change in firm value and the ability to provide a link between the liquidity change and the change in firm value. Private equity placement announcements are studied as they afford the examiner the opportunity to build on prior research in developing a measure of changes in firm value that mollifies the explanatory shadow cast on these changes by the potential resolution of information asymmetries.

The average market response to announcements by firms of decisions to issue equity privately is positive and statistically significant. Disclosing private equity-issue intents between 1988 and 1995, the generally smaller Nasdaq-traded companies experience positive and significant abnormal returns upon announcement.

The preponderance of the evidence in this study suggests that much of the return to a firm at announcement is driven by the firm's size and prospects for growth. Growth prospects are a proxy for liquidity needs and suggest a relationship between the firm's liquidity and market responses. The larger firm is presumed to have less restricted access, on average, to institutional sources of liquidity; if this is the case, a significant negative sign of a firm size factor also supports an optimal liquidity hypothesis. The relationship between market responses and an optimal liquidity hypothesis is further supported by a direct liquidity proxy employed in this study. The change in liquidity measure contributes significantly to the description of announcement period abnormal returns.

Prior research provides some clarity concerning the role played by existing levels of liquidity in describing overall negative market responses to firm announcements of unforeseen issues of equity. An agency costs of free cash flow hypothesis describes certain elements of the adverse reactions and a cash flow signaling hypothesis may describe others. However, this study suggests situations exist where an announcement of an impending equity issue will be received favorably for the firm which is meeting observable needs for liquidity, yet is not possessing excess free cash flow.

4.7.1 *What are the Variables That Effect the Optimal Level of Liquidity and How Do These Factors Impact Market Responses to Liquidity Infusions for the Firm?*

Initial tests of the roles played by varying levels of firm liquidity in explaining market reactions to private equity issue announcements are encouraging. The smaller firm with growth options and observable or stated needs for liquidity appears to possess a higher liquidity optimum. The firms in the sample may, however, have initial levels of liquidity farther from their respective optima than is the norm, thus explaining the positive response. A change in liquidity measure helps to explain market responses to private placement announcements. Contrary to Hertzel and Smith (1993), this examination reveals that firms in financial distress - an indirect proxy for critical liquidity needs - are not significantly favorably treated when they announce private placements. Firms underperforming the market in the weeks prior to the announcements are associated with negative market responses; the implication is that the market has specified a lower liquidity optimum for the underperforming firm than its counterpart.

4.7.2 *Agency Costs of Free Cash Flow Result When Slack is Accumulated Beyond a Firm's Perceived Needs; Empirically, What Are the Implications for Firm Value for the Privately Placing Firm?*

According to the optimal liquidity hypothesis, a firm that is to the left of the optimum in Figure 1 can expect a favorable market response to its receipt of liquidity until the marginal cost of the next dollar of free cash flow offsets the marginal benefits of the next dollar of liquidity. Findings do not, however, uniformly support a free cash flow hypothesis. Test results contrast with average negative market responses to many publicly issuing firms that are "penalized" with an expectation that some portion of the funds received will become free cash flow. Inconsistent with a free cash flow hypothesis, the firms with average existing levels of liquidity are associated with significantly above average market responses.

Overall results in this study prevent direct comment on those firms that may be over-accumulating liquidity and whose returns could be explained by a free cash flow hypothesis. Indirectly, however, the significantly poorer market responses to the larger firm's and low-growth firm's announcements imply an expectation by the market that some portion of those firms' liquidity will not be profitably invested; the larger firm is presumed to have less restricted access to outside liquidity or free cash flow.

Supplementing a free cash flow hypothesis, the firms most strapped for liquidity in this study are not associated with above average responses in the stock market; the firm occupying a range of relative cash availability and enjoying a substantial liquidity infusion is associated with the most positive responses. The capital markets tolerate a higher level of cash accumulation than is suggested in earlier reviews of the implications of cash accumulation on stockholder wealth.

4.8 NOTES

93.   See Section 3.8 for a review of the sample selection procedure.

94.   The positive adjusted and unadjusted abnormal returns in Wruck's study suggest that unexamined factors such as takeover strategies in addition to ownership effects or liquidity resolutions are possibly at play in the firms in her study.

95.   McConnell and Servaes (1995) suggest that private placements of equity are favored for firms with more growth options.

96.   See Morck, Schleifer and Vischny (1988), Melnick and Plaut (1995) and Hertzel and Smith (1993).

97.   Differing firms in differing industries have differing needs for liquidity. A normalization of a firm's possession of liquid resources using SIC codes limits the bias that results from comparing firms in different industries directly to one-another without normalization. However, normalization is accomplished in this study with the adoption of the many other factors that differentiate between firms and industries.

Of the industries in the final sample, only a few "patterns" emerge in the average measures of liquid resources within a given industry. As the number of firms in any given industry increases, the industry normalized measure of liquidity (see Table 1) approaches a universal "norm" of around .35, on average. Several of the industries exhibit a tri-modal distribution of liquidity; a few firms possess inordinate levels of cash and liquid securities and individual measures greater than one, a few others appear insolvent with individual measures less than .1 and a third group occupies a middle ground. The impact of these outliers varies from industry to industry and probably contributes a great deal of "noise" to this variable.

Markets may use liquidity to proxy for the survivability of a firm. In that case, a supplement to Jensen's (1986) proposals is implied. His premise is tempered where a positive return is associated with the firm with some liquidity announcing a liquidity infusion; it is tempered also when markets respond most favorably to the largest infusions of liquidity with the private placements. The premise concerning the over-accumulation of free cash flow by the announcing firm is not supported in this study. No significance can be attached to this hypothesis in any of this study's tests for robustness or cross-sectional explanatory power. The source of this insignificance may be attributable to a preponderance of firms in this study's samples that are not possessing inordinate levels of free cash flow. Privately placing firms may, on average, tend towards inadequate slack and not towards excess free cash flow.

98.   Supplemental factors employed are a "funds use unknown" and "buyer unknown" dummy variable. Neither factor is described in Table 1. Each is adopted to investigate the potential suggested by leaders in the field of finance that the lack of a revelation by the firm of proposed funds use or placement purchaser may invite a significant market response. A negative sign is predicted by the free cash flow hypothesis for firms which are receiving liquid resources, but making no commitment concerning their use. Implications of a "buyer unknown" factor are uncertain. The cross-sectional results of these two factors are not significant. No significant response is attributable to a firm's omission of proposed funds use or buyer identity from its private placement announcement.

99.   Measures adopted in Sections 4.6.2 through 4.6.5 are described in Section 3.9.

100.   Re-estimation follows the procedure outlined in Section 3.2.

CHAPTER 5

Summary, Ideas for Subsequent Research and Concluding Remarks

5.1 The Equity-Issue Puzzle and Firm Liquidity

A current tangent of the equity-issue puzzle is the market's average response to announcements by firms of intents to issue equity privately. A large body of literature documents negative overall market responses to decisions by firms to issue seasoned equity publicly. Several theories are offered to explain these negative responses. A much smaller body of finance research illustrates favorable market responses to news of a firm's plans to issue equity privately.

The equity-issue puzzle, including the free cash flow hypothesis, information theoretic models and ownership structure theory, is supplemented by the findings in the preceding pages. Those findings follow the development of an optimal liquidity hypothesis that is suggested by authors of work dating from the 1960's. Empirical studies since then make few precise allowances for the ability of an optimal liquidity hypothesis to explain returns. Some empirical implications of this hypothesis are proposed in this study. Tests of those implications reveal that an important link exists between market responses to private equity issues, the amount of liquidity provided by those issues and the size and prospects of the firm.

5.2 Summary of Empirical Results

Private equity placement announcements are examined as they provide an opportunity to study changes in firm value independent of issues that may obscure the sources of changes in firm value in other liquidity-enhancing events. The theoretical development of this study considers and its empirical analyses test whether changing levels of firm liquidity help to explain returns observed at the announcement, after controlling for other factors. A change in liquidity measure is constructed that takes into account a firm's size and needs for liquid assets. This measure is significant in describing the cross-section of market responses.

Sixty-nine announcements between 1988 and 1995 are first examined. The firms in this group and in the 67 announcements ultimately considered are relatively small with mean outstanding equity values of less than $70 million and placement sizes averaging approximately $5 million, with a median of $2 million. A traditional event-study methodology is employed with adjustments for the size and per-share price of the equity being privately sold. Significant unadjusted and adjusted positive abnormal returns are discovered over the primary announcement period from three days before until the day of the announcement. Results are similar to responses to private placement announcements observed in prior studies.

Jensen's (1986) free cash flow hypothesis is supplemented with a finding that substantial cash inflows are not necessarily associated with unfavorable market responses for firms issuing equity. Consistent with his premises, the smaller and less diversified firms with greater growth options experience more positive returns upon announcement than their counterparts. Results are consistent with the private buyer delivering positive information to the marketplace with his or her purchase. Tests extend information theoretic models by affirming that proxies for the delivery of new information, and not simply the resolution of management information asymmetries, are significant in describing market responses to firm news.

Ownership structure theory is supplemented with the affirmation that ownership structure is less important in this study, than in similar studies of larger firms, in describing market responses to news of liquidity enhancing events. The suggestion that positive market responses to small-firm events are unrelated to changing ownership concentration is not, however, endorsed. Consistent with prior studies on the relationships between firm value and ownership concentration, changes in ownership concentration pursuant to the private placement are associated with non-monotonic changes in firm value. At intermediate levels of ownership concentration between 5 and 25% of outstanding shares, increasing concentration is associated with negative adjusted abnormal returns. Increases in concentration above and below this intermediate level are associated with positive (p-values equal .119 and .168, respectively), albeit insignificant, market responses.

Proxies for growth opportunities and firm size are robust in explaining the overall positive returns. These two variables' levels of significance are unaffected by any of the issues that diminish the explanatory power of other factors employed by this study.

A proxy for restricted or unregistered shares is not significant. This contrasts with earlier studies attributing positive significance to this variable. The less liquid firms are observed more frequently issuing unregistered shares than the more liquid ones. The less liquid firms receive the more adverse market response and this relationship adds to the "insignificance" of the restricted shares factor. It is noteworthy, however, that many of the Rule 144-A and Regulation S issues which can be resold to "qualified institutional buyers" absent SEC approval are non-domestic and are excluded from this study's final sample. Attaching any great importance to this discovery is therefore tenuous.

Abnormal returns are conditioned by changes in liquidity. More positive market responses are associated with larger changes in liquidity. Findings are consistent with firms in the sample occupying a range of liquidity levels to the left of the optima in Figures 1–4, according to an optimal liquidity hypothesis. The size of the change or, considered independently, existing liquidity levels, may proxy for firm survivability. Similarly, a significant and adverse response is observed for the firm underperforming the market in the weeks prior to the announcement. The firm whose vulnerable financial condition is evidenced by either performance below market averages or by low levels of liquidity is one that encounters a negative market response, on average, to its private placement plans.

5.3 Extensions and Implications for Subsequent Research

The purpose of this study is not to test for the strength of all possible explanations for returns observed upon announcement of private placements of equity. A framework is merely used in the preceding chapters to begin the discovery of the part played by firm liquidity in influencing these firm re-valuations. This discovery, in turn, serves as a catalyst for later research.

Jensen (1986) suggests that management reputation is important in explaining positive market responses. He proposes that non-negative returns accrue especially to the firms that the market "trusts" to not waste arriving liquidity, whatever its source. A later test of stock-price behavior upon announcement of private equity placements might include an allowance for management reputation. This can be accomplished through the use of measures of firm diversity, for example, where a management with a history of focused and undiversified investment receives more positive market responses, on average, to its security-issue announcements.

Management resistance to firm exit might include a private placement of equity to postpone exit. A period of financial distress can generally be expected to precede these firms' exits if management has been resisting those exits. A private placement can be part of this resistance strategy and be recognized as such by the capital markets. The distressed firm suffers a negative market response to the private placement announcement. Stock market participants discount firm value given an increased expectation that management is merely denying the inevitable and is being afforded additional opportunity by the private placement to further waste corporate resources. New studies of changes in firm value at announcement can allow for this by examining the long-run performance of the issuing firms. A test is contemplated for the degree to which the market anticipates the exit of some of the announcing firms.

Among the factors best describing the cross-section of market responses to private placement announcement is firm size. The ability of firm size to describe also a firm's optimal level of liquidity is unclear. Test results imply the larger firm has a lower relative need for liquidity. A presumption exists that the larger firms have greater relative access to borrowing and, on average, longer term relationships with lenders. This access describes an unknown portion of a firm's "liquidity." Subsequent study can investigate the manner with which firm size helps to describe both the firm's "real" levels of liquidity and the firm's effective level of optimal liquidity.

Therefore, questions to be considered include:

1. What is the significance of firm size in investors' beliefs about the firm's available liquidity?

An extensive literature describes the inverse relationship that exists, on average, between firm size and stock returns. The relation between firm size and liquidity is less clear. Are more adverse market responses to larger firm announcements due, in part, to the market's perception that the larger firm is in lesser need of new liquidity than its smaller counterpart? A simple price-per-share measure, used by Bhardwaj and Brooks (1999), may begin to address elements of this question.

2. What is the power of the liquidity measure in anticipating firm survival? And purely as a statistical issue, how can the means and standard deviations of a firm's levels of existing and arriving liquidity be used to describe variations in market responses to these private placement announcements?

Reference is made in this study to the potential of liquidity and underperformance measures proxying for firm survival. A simple test can examine the survivorship of the privately placing firms in the intermediate and long term. If the change in liquidity and underperformance measures anticipate survival, then the underperforming firms in this study will have a lower rate of survival than better-performing firms or those with more substantial levels of arriving liquidity.

3. If liquidity helps to characterize market responses to private placements, should it also characterize returns to all general cash offerings?

The importance of liquidity and changes in liquidity in describing market responses to all general cash offerings is not clear. The robustness of an optimal liquidity hypothesis to general cash offerings can be tested by examining public issues. If the premise is robust, then similar outcomes for liquidity proxies will be observed with the public as with the private sample.

4. What is the impact of successively more relaxed SEC guidelines on the resale of private placements?

Earlier studies generate results consistent with the premise that the purchase of restricted stock is a solid vote of confidence by the buyer. With the assumption of an illiquid stake, the buyer must contribute to, or disproportionately believe in, the prospects of the firm. This vote of confidence is diminished where the buyer can resell, under new SEC guidelines, unregistered or restricted stock. A sample of private placement announcements prior to and after the regulatory changes can be examined to test the strength of hypotheses varying with regulatory dictum.

5. When might a firm prefer a private placement over other external financing sources?

Allowing the decision by the firm, or appropriateness for the firm, to make a private placement to be the dependent variable, a logit model can characterize the probability that a given firm should issue privately vs. publicly. Empirically and theoretically, how do a firm's available liquidity and needs for liquidity influence its preference for privately procured financing? Public and private issues are examined. Extending Myers and Majluf's (1984) underinvestment dilemma, such factors as firm size, recent performance, ownership structure, the size of the liquidity needs and pre-issue levels of liquidity should describe the selection of private or public markets.

6. What is the source of the discount granted to the buyers in this study?

The study by Hertzel and Smith (1993) attributes much of the discount afforded private placement buyers to information releases the buyers provide and expenses incurred by the buyers in gathering information for their purchase. The discount granted on average in Wruck's (1989) private placement study is small and suggests her sample is populated by firms later acquired in tandem with the private placement buyers. The discounts in this

study are similar to Hertzel and Smith's (1993). A test is anticipated that examines firm performance in the years following the
private placement announcement to examine acquisition activity
and to examine firm survivorship, as well.

7.   Finally, what do this study's results portend concerning the
     relevance of one or another theory of capital structure?

Studies by Opler, Pinkowitz, Stulz and Williamson (1999) and
Shyam-Sunder and Myers (1999) consider firm choice of liquidity
levels and suggest support for the static-tradeoff and pecking
order theories of capital structure, respectively. This study lends
greater support to a pecking order model. Later study contem-
plates further examination of this topic.

5.4 Concluding Remarks

A link exists between liquidity and market responses to news of
the firm's intent to issue privately. This study holds that adverse
market responses to the typical equity placement announcement
are tempered where a firm has an observable need for liquidity to
meet operating needs or pursue profitable investment. The
strength of this proposal is considered in the context of a liquidity
changing event and an observable change in firm value.

A pattern of statistically significant positive responses to private
equity-issue announcements is observed. The size of the liquidity-
enhancement from the private placement plays a significant part
in explaining the returns. An extension of the optimal liquidity
hypothesis suggests that included liquidity proxies in a modeling
of market responses to security issues may assist management in
predicting the consequences of a new issue announcement.
Coupling these results with prior theoretical and empirical work
describing the costs of liquidity and the implications of financing choices provides fruitful prospects for later research.

Security Regulations and Private Placements[1]

A. Security Issue Background

A review of existing securities regulations in the United States follows. These regulations are founded on the Securities Act of 1933 (the Act) and the Securities Exchange Act of 1934. The Act governs the issuance of new securities; its rules dictate the legal framework for the private placements of equity at the federal level and are supplemented by rules in the individual states. Individual state rules are not examined in this appendix.

The basic and guiding principle of securities regulation in the United States is an avoidance of the sorts of financial debacles which surrounded the 1929 crash; this avoidance, according to Congressional intent, should be accomplished without onerous and costly interferences with the conduct of business. Congress passed the Act to protect investors from "fraud and misrepresentation in the public offering, trading, voting and tendering of securities." Section 5 of the Act is integral to the achievement of the Act's primary mission of protecting the investor from duplicitous issuers. This section mandates extensive and costly informational filings with the Securities and Exchange Commission (SEC) before new securities can be sold to the public. The SEC makes no guarantees whatsoever as to the appropriateness of one new security issue or another; it merely attests to the fulfilment of reporting requirements by the prospective issuer. The only way an issuer can legally avoid these costly frictions and circumvent these reporting requirements is with a sale directly to an informed purchaser or small group of purchasers (the number varies form state to state); these unregistered - and subsequently not exchange or Nasdaq tradeable - securities are known as private placements since they occur directly between the issuer and the purchaser; however, not all securities placed directly with a purchaser by the issuer are necessarily unregistered and restricted. Some private placements are of "conventional" securities which otherwise conform to the reporting requirements of Section 5 of the Act. The shelf registration allowances, for example, provide a manner with which a firm - depending on the provisions of its charter - can place "normal" equity with a private purchaser. A private placement, in line with U. S. Securities law and for purposes of this study, is "a security that is issued in the United States but is exempt from registration with the Securities and Exchange Commission as a result of being issued in transactions not involving any public offering."

The public issuer suffers a number of costs as he or she brings a security to the market. These costs generally include SEC filing fees, underwriter fees, printing costs, accounting and attorney fees and rating fees for debt-type issues. Acknowledging the costliness of bringing a public issue through the regulatory matrix, the SEC provides exemptions from the registration requirements of Section 5 for certain transactions in which "investors are capable of protecting themselves." These "certain transactions" include private placements.

B. The Private Placement Market

The SEC recognizes that "direct negotiations between investors and issuers" provide ample opportunity for the prospective purchasers to safeguard their interests. As noted in the text of this study and in the majority of the private placement announcements, most private placement purchasers are large individual or institutional investors who can be reasonably expected to adequately protect themselves in a manner analogous to the protections provided by Section 5 of the Act.[2]

B.1 *Advantages of the Private Placement Market*

The privately placed security offers several distinct advantages. First, Section 5 registration costs are reduced.[3] The private placement negotiated directly between issuers and investors typically avoids many legal, accounting, financial intermediary - and all regulatory - fees. Second, the placement can be quickly brought to market and can avoid the lengthy registration process; a private placement can often be completed in weeks or even days vs. the months-long Section 5 protocol.

A third advantage to the issuer or the purchaser wishing to remain private is the exemption from detailed disclosure provided by the privately placed and purchased security. Section 5 orders an exhaustive provision of detailed financial data by the issuing firm and substantial disclosures by purchasers of interests exceeding 5% of publicly traded firms. These disclosures are bypassed with the private placement by the publicly traded firm whose by-laws make provision for the private issue of equity or whose private issue has been approved by stockholders.

A final advantage of the private placement is its ability to be custom-tailored for both the issuer and the purchaser. Whether meeting the needs of a highly levered firm or an investor with a special set of investment return requirements, the private placement lends itself more easily than do public placement in meeting these unique needs. The private market may provide funds-of-last-resort to the distressed firm, funds for the firm with otherwise illiquid publicly traded securities or funds to meet some unusual capital investment horizon.

B.2 *Disadvantages of the private placement market*

Until the advent of Rule 144-A - discussed below - the most glaring disadvantage of privately placed equity was the preclusion of its resale. Given that the typical private placement of equity is structured absent the reporting requirements of Section 5 of the Act, it only follows that the resale of privately placed securities - in markets referenced by Section 5 - is prohibited.

A second drawback of the private placement is an expectation that the private purchaser will generally require a higher return than the public issue purchaser. Financing is often more restrictive to the issuer. The reduced liquidity and presumably greater risks assumed by the private placement purchaser allow that purchaser to extract a risk and illiquidity premium. The issuer is often restrained by covenants in the private placement that reduce his or her flexibility in financial and strategic policymaking.

C. Rule 144-A and Private Placement Resale

The SEC adopted in 1990 a special rule - now known as Rule 144-A (the rule)-that exempts certain purchasers of securities from the reporting requirements of Section 5 of the Act. The rule was first proposed in 1988. It allows "qualified institutional buyers" (QIB's) to engage in the resale and purchase of securities otherwise exempt from registration under the Act.[4] The rule requires that the seller notify the purchaser of the restricted nature of the securities offered, that the securities not be of the same class as securities listed on a national exchange or the Nasdaq, and that the purchaser be granted reasonable access to information on the issuer. Similar disclosures to subsequent purchasers of the unregistered shares are required to be made by the initial purchaser and/or the issuing firm. Although a secondary market existed before the rule's adoption in 1990, its legality and structure were not clear.[5]

D. Implications of Section 5, the Act, Rule 144-A and Regulation S

Examinations of the stockholder wealth effects of the announcements of private placements of equity have been complicated by the importance of the restricted status of issued securities in explaining the cross-section of observed returns. A presumption exists that where the purchased security is restricted and "opportunistic resale" is prevented following a discounted purchase, a more meaningful and favorable signal is being provided by the purchaser to the capital markets. However, given the ability of even restricted and unregistered stock to be resold to a "sophisticated" and informed large investor, the meaningfulness of this unregistered status is reduced relative to studies which preceded the adoptions of Rule 144-A and Regulation S in 1990.

The results provided in studies prior to the adoption of these more generous resale regulations are probably suspect if they are used to describe more recent unregistered or restricted issues.

A variable describing the exempt status of private placements after 1990 is probably today much less significant (and potentially neutral) than before 1990. Additionally, as noted by Foerster and Karolyi (1998), the SEC is now investigating the potential abuse of Rule 144-A in the circumnavigation of United States securities regulations. This circumnavigation may lead to the curtailment of Rule 144-A by the SEC and a new set of rules for international private placement buyers and sellers in the near future.

E. NOTES

1. The discussion in this Appendix is taken from the Securities Act of 1933, as amended through 1996, and a treatise provided by Lisa Bostwick in the Winter 1996 issue of *Law and Policy in International Business.*

2. Recall that institutional ownership of U. S. Equities has grown from less than one-third in 1975 to the vast majority of outstanding shares today.

3. According to Bostwick (1996), these costs may be reduced by two thirds vs. a public placement of a similar dollar-sized issue.

4. QIB's are defined as "entities owning and investing at least $100 million in securities." These are not necessarily "institutions" in the strictest sense. A large individual investor can be considered a QIB. The scope of the definition is broad enough to include "life insurance companies, pension funds, investment companies (mutual funds), foreign and domestic banks, savings and loan associations and master and collective trusts." For a dealer to participate in the acquisition or resale of these otherwise exempt securities, that dealer had first to own or invest in on a discretionary basis at "least $10 million in unaffiliated securities."

5. The existence of this secondary market, especially overseas, was recognized by the SEC in its creation of Rule 144-A. Regulation S was issued "contemporaneously with Rule 144-A." This regulation allows the flow-back to the United States of privately placed domestic securities purchased abroad. It "provides for the resale of unregistered securities outside the United States and marks the end of the SEC's attempt to regulate the overseas purchase of unregistered securities by U. S. nationals."

Bibliography

Akerlof, G. A., 1970, The market for lemons: Quality and the market mechanism, *Quarterly Journal of Economics* 84:488–500.

Ambarish, R., K. John, and J. Williams, 1987, Efficient signalling with dividends and investments, *Journal of Finance* 42:321–343.

Amihud, Y., B. Lev, and N. G. Travlos, 1990, Corporate control and the choice of investment financing: The case of corporate acquisitions, *Journal of Finance* 45:603–616.

Ang, J., 1991, The corporate slack controversy, *Advances in Working Capital Management* by JAI Press, Inc. 2:3–14.

Asquith, P. and D. W. Mullins, Jr., 1986a, Equity issues and offering dilution, *Journal of Financial Economics* 15:61–89.

Asquith, P. and D. W. Mullins, 1986b, Signalling with dividends, stock repurchases and equity issues, *Financial Management* 15:27–44.

Bagnani, E., N. Milonas, A. Saunders and N. Travlos, 1994, Managers, owners, and the pricing of risky debt: an empirical analysis, *Journal of Finance* 49:453–477.

Barclay, M. J. and C. G. Holderness, 1989, Private benefits from control of public corporations, *Journal of Financial Economics* 25:371–395.

Barclay, M. J. and R. H. Litzenberger, 1988, Announcement effects of new equity issues and the use of intraday price data, *Journal of Financial Economics* 21:71–99.

Barron, R. A., 1995, Control and restricted securities, *Securities Regulation Law Journal* 23:320–324.

Baxter, N. and J. Cragg, 1970, Corporate choice among long-term financing instruments, *Review of Economics and Statistics* 52:225–235.

Bayless, M., 1994, The influence of predictability on differences in the market reaction to debt and equity issue announcements, *Journal of Financial Research* 17:117–131.

Bayless, M. and S. Chaplinsky, 1996, Is there a window of opportunity for seasoned equity issuance?, *Journal of Finance* 51:253–278.

Bayless, M. E. and D. J. Diltz, 1991, The relevance of asymmetric information to financing decisions, *Journal of Business Finance And Accounting* 18:331–344.

Bayless, M. E. and D. J. Diltz, 1994, Security offerings and capital structure theory, *Journal of Business Finance And Accounting* 21:77–91.

Beranek, W., C. Cornwell and S. Choi, 1995, External financing, liquidity, and capital expenditures, *Journal of Financial Research,* 18:207–222.

Berle, A. A., Jr. and G. C. Means, 1932, *The Modern Corporation and Private Property,* New York: Macmillan.

Bhagat, S., J. A. Brickley and R. C. Lease, 1986, The authorization of additional common stock, *Financial Management* 15:45–53.

Billingsley, R. S., R. E. Lamy and D. M. Smith, 1990, Units of debt with warrants: Evidence of the penalty-free issuance of an equity-like security, *Journal of Financial Research* 13:187–199.

Blackwell, D. W. and D. S. Kidwell, 1988, An investigation of the cost differences between public sales and private placements of debt, *Journal of Financial Economics* 22:253–278.

Bostwick, L. A., 1996, The SEC response to internationalization and institutionalization: Rule 144-A merit regulation of investors, *Law and Policy in International Business* 27:423–445.

Bradford, W., 1987, The issue decision of manager owners under information asymmetry, *Journal of Finance* 42:1245–1260.

Brennan, M. and A. Kraus, 1987, Efficient financing under asymmetric information, *Journal of Finance* 42:1225–1243.

Brickley, J. A., R. C. Lease, and C. W. Smith, Jr., 1988, Ownership structure and voting on antitakeover amendments, *Journal of Financial Economics* 20:267–291.

Brous, P. A., 1992, Common stock offerings and earnings expectations: A test of the release of unfavorable information, *Journal of Finance* 47:1517-1536.

Brous, P. A. and O. Kini, 1992, Equity issues and Tobin's Q: New evidence regarding alternative information release hypotheses, *Journal of Financial Research* 15: 323–339.

Bugeja, M. and T. Walter, 1995, An empirical analysis of some determinants of the target shareholder premium in takeovers, *Accounting and Finance* 35:33–60.

Carey, M., S. Prouse, J. Rea and G. Udell, 1994, The economics of the private placement market, *Federal Reserve Bulletin* 80:5–6.

Cooney, J. W. and A. Kalay, 1993, Positive information from equity issue announcements, *Journal of Financial Economics* 33:149–172.

Cornett, M. M. and H. Tehranian, 1994, An examination of voluntary versus involuntary security issuances by commercial banks: The impact of capital regulations on common stock returns, *Journal of Financial Economics* 35:99–122.

Crutchley, C. E., C. D. Hudson and M. R. H. Jensen, 1994/1995, Corporate earnings and financings: An analysis of cancelled versus completed offerings, *Journal of Applied Business Research* 11: 46–59.

Davis, S., 1990, Information management: The wiring of 144A, *Institutional Investor* 24: 219–220.

Demsetz, H., 1983, The structure of ownership and the theory of the firm, *Journal of Law and Economics* 26:375–390.

Demsetz, H. and K. Lehn, 1985, The structure of corporate ownership: Causes and consequences, *Journal of Political Economy* 93:1155–1177.

Denis, D. J., 1994, Investment opportunities and the market reaction to equity offerings, *Journal of Financial and Quantitative Analysis* 29:159-177.

Diamond, D., 1985, Optimal release of information by the firm, *Journal of Finance* 40:1071–1094.

Dierkens, N., 1991, Information asymmetry and equity issues, *Journal of Financial and Quantitative Analysis* 26:181–199.

Diltz, J. D., L. J. Lockwood and S. Min, 1992, Sources of wealth loss in new equity issues, *Journal of Banking and Finance* 16:511–522.

Doran, D. T., 1994, Stock splits: Tests of the earnings signalling and attention directing hypotheses, *Journal of Accounting, Auditing and Finance* 9:411–422.

Easterbrook, F., 1984, Two-agency cost explanations of dividends, *American Economic Review* 74:650–659.

Eisenbeis, R. A., 1977, Pitfalls in the application of discriminant analysis in business, finance and economics, *Journal of Finance* 32:875–900.

Fama, E. F. and K. French, 1992, The cross-section of expected returns, *Journal of Finance* 47:427–465.

Fama, E. F. and M. C. Jensen, 1983, Separation of ownership and control, *Journal of Law and Economics* 26:301–325.

Ferreira, E.J. and L. Brooks, 1999, Evidence on equity private placements and going-out-of-business information release, *Journal of Economics and Business* 51: 377-394.

Fields, L. P. and E. L. Mais, 1994, Managerial voting rights and seasoned public equity issues, *Journal of Financial and Quantitative Analysis* 29:445–457.

Fields, L.P. and E. L. Mais, 1991, The valuation effects of private placements of convertible debt, *Journal of Finance* 46:1925–1932.

Foerster, S. R. and G. A. Karolyi, 1998, The long run performance of global equity offerings, Working Paper, Richard Ivey School of Business, University of Western Ontario.

Frankel, R., M. McNichols and G. P. Wilson, 1995, Discretionary disclosure and external financing, *Accounting Review* 70:135–150.

Gilson, S. C., K. John, and L. P. Lang, 1990, Troubled debt restructurings: An empirical study of private reorganization of firms in default, *Journal of Finance Economics* 27:315–353.

Glasky, J. H., 1989, Rule 144A: A quiet revolution in private placements, *Journal of Accountancy* 168:68–72.

Goldfeld, S. M. and R. E. Quandt, 1976, Techniques for estimating switching regressions, in *Studies in Non-linear Estimation,* pp. 3–37, Ballinger Publishing Company.

Greene, W. H., *Econometric Analysis,* Second Edition, 1993, MacMillan Press.

Griggs, F. T., D. M. Kim and R. L. Smith, 1995, Announcement and publication decisions and the use of prediction errors in cross-sectional analysis: Evidence on seasonal equity issues, *Financial Review* 30: 139–174.

Hansen, R. and C. Crutchley, 1990, Corporate earnings and financing: An empirical analysis, *Journal of Business* 63:347–371.

Harris, M. and A. Raviv, 1988, Corporate control contests and capital structure, *Journal of Financial Economics* 20:55–86.

Harris, M. and A. Raviv, 1991, The theory of capital structure, *Journal of Finance* 46:297–355.

Healy, P. M. and K. G. Palepu, 1990, Earnings and risk changes surrounding primary stock offers, *Journal of Accounting Research* 28: 25–48.

Healy, P. and K. Palepu, 1993, The effect of firm financial disclosure strategies on stock prices, *Accounting Horizons* 7:1–11.

Hertzel, M. and R. L. Smith, 1993, Market discounts and shareholder gains from placing equity privately, *Journal of Finance* 48:459–485.

Holderness, C. G. and D. D. Sheehan, 1985, Raiders or saviors: The evidence on six controversial investors, *Journal of Financial Economics* 14:555–579.

Holderness, C. and D. Sheehan, 1988, The role of majority shareholders in publicly held corporations: An exploratory analysis, *Journal of Financial Economics* 20:317–346.

Huberman, G., 1984, External financing and liquidity, *Journal of Finance* 34:895–910.

Hull, R. M., 1994, Stock price behavior of pure capital structure issuance and cancellation announcements, *Journal of Financial Research* 17: 439–448.

Hull, R. M. and R. Moellenberndt, 1994, Bank debt reduction announcements and negative signalling, *Financial Management* 23:21–30.

James, C., 1987, Some evidence on the uniqueness of bank loans, *Journal of Financial Economics* 19:217–235.

Jensen, M. C., 1986, Agency costs of free cash flow, corporate finance and takeovers, *American Economic Review* 76:323–329.

Jensen, M. C. and W. H. Meckling, 1976, Theory of the firm: Managerial behavior, agency costs, and ownership structure, *Journal of Financial Economics* 3:305–360.

Jensen, M. C. and J. B. Warner, 1988, The distribution of power among corporate managers, shareholders and directors, *Journal of Financial Economics* 20:3–24.

Johnson, D., J. Serrano and R. Thompson, 1996, Seasoned equity offerings for new investment and the information content of insider trades, *Journal of Financial Research* 19:91–103.

Kalay, A. and A. Shimrat, 1987, Firm value and seasoned equity issues: Price pressure, wealth redistribution, or negative information, *Journal of Financial Economics* 19:109–126.

Kane, E. J. and H. Unal, 1990, Modeling structural and temporal variation in the markets's valuation of banking firms, *Journal of Finance* 45:113–136.

Kenworthy, M. W., 1993, How emerging growth companies can find financing, *Corporate Cashflow* 14:47–48.

Kennedy, P. K., *A Guide to Econometrics*, Third Edition, 1992, The MIT Press.

Kershaw, T., 1994, The maturing of the private market, *Investment Dealer's Digest*, August 22, 1994:12–21.

Kolodny, R. and D. R. Suhler, 1988, The effects of new debt issues on existing security holders, *Quarterly Journal of Business and Economics* 27:51–72.

Lehn, K. and A. Poulsen, 1989, Free cash flow and stockholder gain in going private transactions, *Journal of Finance* 44:771–787.

Leland, H. E. and D. H. Pyle, 1977, Information asymmetries, financial structure and financial intermediation, *Journal of Finance* 32:371–387.

Lerner, J., 1994, Venture capitalists and the decision to go public, *Journal of Financial Economics* 35:293–316.

Loderer, C. F. and D. C. Mauer, 1992, Corporate dividends and seasoned equity issues, *Journal of Finance* 47:201–225.

Loderer, C. F., D. Sheehan and G. Kadlec, 1991, The pricing and equity offerings, *Journal of Financial Economics* 29:35–57.

Loughran, T. and J. R. Ritter, 1995, The new issues puzzle, *Journal of Finance* 50:23–51.

Lucas, D. J. and R. L. McDonald, 1990, Equity issues and stock price dynamics, *Journal of Finance* 45:1019–1043.

Lummer, S. L. and J. J. McConnell, 1989, Further evidence on the bank lending process and the capital-market response to bank loan agreements, *Journal of Financial Economics* 25:99–122.

Mann, S. V. and N. W. Sicherman, 1991, The agency costs of free cash flow: Acquisition activity and equity issues, *Journal of Business* 64: 213–227.

Marsh, P., 1982, The choice between equity and debt: An empirical study, *Journal of Finance* 37:121–144.

Martin, J. and D. Scott, A discriminant analysis of the corporate debt-equity decision, *Financial Management* 3:71–79.

Masulis, R. W. and A. N. Korwar, 1986, Seasoned equity offerings: An empirical investigation, *Journal of Financial Economics* 15:91–118.

McConnell, J. and C. Muscarella, 1985, Corporate capital expenditure decisions and the market value of the firm, *Journal of Financial Economics* 14:399–422.

McConnell, J. and H. Servaes, 1990, Additional evidence on equity ownership and corporate value, *Journal of Financial Economics* 27:595–612.

McConnell, J. and H. Servaes, 1995, Equity ownership and the two faces of debt, *Journal of Financial Economics* 39:131–157.

Melnik, A. L. and S. E. Plaut, 1995, Disclosure costs, regulation and the expansion of the private placement market: Professional adaptation, *Journal of Accounting, Auditing and Finance* 10:23–42.

Mikkelson, W. H. and M. M. Partch, 1986, Valuation effects of security offerings and the issuance process, *Journal of Financial Economics* 15: 31–60.

Mikkelson, W. and M. M. Partch, 1988, Withdrawn security offerings, *Journal of Financial and Quantitative Analysis* 23:119–133.

Mikkelson, W. H. and R. S. Ruback, 1985, An empirical analysis of the interfirm equity investment process, *Journal of Financial Economics* 14:523–553.

Miller, M. H. and D. Orr, 1966, A model of the demand for money by firms, *Quarterly Journal of Economics* 80:413–435.

Miller, M. H. and D. Orr, 1968, The demand for money by firms: Extensions of analytic results, *Journal of Finance* 23:735–759.

Miller, M. H. and K. Rock, 1985, Dividend policy under asymmetric information, *Journal of Finance* 40:1031–1051.

Milligan, J. W., 1990, Two cheers for 144A, *Institutional Investor* 24: 117–119.

Morck, R., A. Shleifer and R. W. Vishny, 1988, Management ownership and market valuation: An empirical analysis, *Journal of Financial Economics* 20:293–315.

Myers, A. D., 1992, Syndicated private offerings add equity to emerging companies, *Corporate Cashflow* 13:28–30.

Myers, S. C., 1977, Determinants of corporate borrowing, *Journal of Financial Economics* 5:147–175.

Myers, S. C., 1993, Still Searching for the Optimal Capital Structure, *Journal of Applied Corporate Finance* 6:4-14.

Myers, S. C. and N. S. Majluf, 1984, Corporate financing and investment decisions when firms have information that investors do not have, *Journal of Financial Economics* 13:187–221.

Officer, D. T. and R. L. Smith, 1986, Announcement effects of withdrawn security offerings, *Journal of Financial Research* 9:229–238.

Opler, T., L. Pinkowitz, R. Stulz and R. Williamson, 1999, The determinants and implications of corporate cash holdings, *Journal of Financial Economics* 52:3–46.

Park, S. and M. Song, 1995, Employee stock ownership plans, firm performance and monitoring by outside blockholders, *Financial Management* 24:52–65.

Parsons, J. and A. Raviv, 1985, Underpricing of seasoned issues, *Journal of Financial Economics* 14:377–397.

Perfect, S. B., D. Peterson and P. Peterson, 1995, Self-tender offers: the effect of free cash flow, cash flow signalling and the measurement of Tobin's Q, *Journal of Banking and Finance* 19:1005–1023.

Pilotte, E., 1992, Growth opportunities and the stock price response to new financing, *Journal of Business* 65:371–394.

Raad, E. and R. Ryan, 1995, Capital structure and ownership distribution of tender offer targets: An empirical study, *Financial Management,* 24:46–56.

Ross, S. A., 1977, The determination of financial structure: The incentive signalling approach, *Bell Journal of Economics* 8:23–40.

Sant, R. and S. P. Ferris, 1994, Seasoned equity offerings: The case of all-equity firms, *Journal of Business, Finance and Accounting* 21:429–444.

Sant, R. and H. Thiewes, 1995, Stock splits and equity issues: An empirical investigation, Mankato State Univesity working paper.

Schadler, F. P. and W. T. Moore, 1992, The effects of predictability on stock price response to the financing decision, *Journal of Business, Finance and Accounting* 19:865–875.

Schipper, K. and A. Smith, 1986, A comparison of equity carve outs and seasoned equity offerings: Share price effects and corporate restructuring, *Journal of Financial Economics* 15:153–186.

Sherman, A. J., 1991, Private placements, *D&B Reports* 39:46.

Shleifer, A. and R. Vishny, 1986, Large shareholders and corporate control, *Journal of Political Economy* 95:461–488.

Shyam-Sunder, L. and S. C. Myers, 1999, Testing static tradeoff against pecking order models of capital structure, *Journal of Financial Economics* 51:219–44.

Slovin, M. B., M. E. Sushka and Y. M. Bendeck, 1994, Seasoned common stock issuance following an IPO, *Journal of Banking and Finance* 18: 207–226.

Smith, C. W., Jr., 1986, Investment banking and the capital acquisition process, *Journal of Financial Economics* 15:3–29.

Smith, C. and R. Watts, 1992, The investment opportunity set and corporate financing, dividend and compensation policies, *Journal of Financial Economics* 32:263–292.

Smith, M. S., 1991, Continued growth is likely for private placement mart, *Investment Dealers Digest* 57:29:24–25.

Smith, R. L. and J. Kim, 1994, The combined effects of free cash flow and financial stock on bidder and target stock returns, *Journal of Business* 67:281–310.

Speiss, D. K. and J. Affleck-Graves, 1995, Under-performance in long-run stock returns following seasoned equity offerings, *Journal of Financial Economics* 38:243–267.

Stein, J. C., 1992, Convertible bonds as backdoor equity financing, *Journal of Financial Economics* 32:3–21.

Stevens, M., 1988, Private placements can finance your business, *D&B Reports* 36:46–47.

Stulz, R. M., 1988, Managerial control of voting rights: Financing policies and the market for corporate control, *Journal of Financial Economics* 20:25–54.

Stulz, R. M., 1990, Managerial discretion and optimal financing policies, *Journal of Financial Economics* 26:3–27.

Sun, H. L., 1995, Investment opportunities, information asymmetry and the valuation effect of debt announcements, *American Business Review* 13:39–49.

Taub, A. J., 1975, Determinants of the firm's capital structure, *Review of Economics and Statistics* 57:410–416.

Tucker, L. and M. Long, 1994, Why a private offering pays, *Corporate Finance* 119:32–35.

Varma, R. and S. H. Szewczyk, 1993, The private placement of bank equity, *Journal of Banking and Finance* 17:1111–1131.

Viswanath, P. V., 1993, Strategic considerations, the pecking order hypothesis and market reactions to equity financing, *Journal of Financial and Quantitative Analysis* 28:213–234.

Vogt, S. C., 1994, The cash flow-investment relationship: Evidence from U.S. manufacturing firms, *Financial Management* 23:3–20.

Wruck, K. H., 1989, Equity ownership concentration and firm value: Evidence from private equity financings, *Journal of Financial Economics* 23:3–28.

Yorks, R. A., 1990, A hurray for 144-A, *Institutional Investor* 24:86–87.

Table 1 Variable Definitions

Liquidity/ Change in Liquidity	Liquidity is liquid assets divided by funds required for preferred dividends and current operating and debt servicing needs. Change in liquidity is the change in the liquidity measure resulting from the private placement divided by the liquidity measure before the private placement. Current is defined as the most recently reported year prior to the announcement of the private placement. Liquid assets are the sum of cash plus accounts receivable plus short term marketable securities. Reference is the sum of Annual Data Items numbered 162, 2 and 193 from pages 5–32, 5–203 and 5–240 of the 1994 User's Guide of *Compustat*, respectively. Funds required for preferred dividends and current operating and debt servicing needs equal the sum of preferred dividends plus interest expense plus current maturities of debt plus costs of goods sold plus selling and administrative expenses. Reference is the sum of Annual Data Items numbered 19, 15, 44, 41 and 189. These are drawn, respectively, from pages 5–82, 5–132, 5–62, 5–49 and 5–239 of the User's Guide.
Earnings/Price	Proxied by the ratio of earnings per share to market price five days before the first announcement of the private placement. Specifically, this is Primary Earnings Per Share Excluding Extraordinary Items divided by the stock price at day −3. Reference is Annual Data Item Number 58 from page 5–88 of the User's Guide divided by the market price taken from the CRSP tapes.
New Product	1 if the financial press indicates the private placement will be used to fund a speculative new product and 0 otherwise. Language is examined in each private placement announcement. Where it is unclear whether funds from the private placement will be invested in a "new product", this variable takes on a 0 value.

Table 1 (Continued)

Working Capital	1 if the private placement proceeds are reported in the financial press as intended by the firm to be used for working capital and 0 otherwise. Language in each private placement announcement is scrutinized to determine the firm's intent. When it is unclear whether the use is for working capital, this variable takes on a 0 value.
Single/Foreign Investor	1 if the placement is sold to a single/foreign buyer and 0 otherwise. Language is studied in each announcement to see whether an individual/foreign or group of foreign investors is buying the private placement. A single investor can be only an individual human being and not a single institutional investor or corporation. Where buyer unity or origin is unclear, this variable takes on a 0 value.
Management Buyer	1 if a manager or director is the buyer or if the buyer is friendly to or controlled by management and 0 otherwise. Language is examined further to discover if the control adjacent to the purchased and privately placed shares will fall into management or management-friendly hands. If the loyalty of the purchaser to management or outsiders is unclear, this variable takes on a 0 value.
Ownership Concentration Level 1	1 if management ownership after the placement is between 0% and 5% and 0 otherwise. "Management ownership" includes beneficial control by management of voting shares and common stock ownership by shareholders noted as loyal to management in either the private placement announcement or SEC reports as provided by *Compaq Disclosure*. The most recent *Compaq Disclosure* report prior to the private placement announcement is used to determine management ownership after the announcement as the sum of the earlier *Compaq Disclosure* ownership report and the amount purchased in the private placement.

Table 1 (Continued)

Ownership Concentration Level 2	1 if management ownership after the placement is between 5% and 25% and 0 otherwise. "Management ownership" is measured in this level in a manner analogous to that used for Ownership Concentration Level 1.
Ownership Concentration Level 3	1 if management ownership after the placement is over 25% and 0 otherwise. "Management ownership" is measured in this level in a manner analogous to that used for Ownership Concentration Level 1.
Financial Distress	1 if the firm has had 2 consecutive years of negative earnings and 0 otherwise. Reference is the Annual Data Item number 118 from page 5–116 of the User's Guide. This is the Restated Income Before Extraordinary Items.
Restricted Shares	1 if the shares to be placed are identified as restricted or unregistered and 0 otherwise. A search is made of the private placement announcement for the words "restricted" or "unregistered"; if the SEC registration status of the placement is not noted or is unclear, this variable takes on a 0 value.
Prior Underperformance	1 if the firm's raw returns over the event period (−59, −10) are below the average for the value-weighted index. This variable takes on a 0 value for all other firms. Returns are calculated using the CRSP daily returns file. A holding period return is calculated for each firm over the period (−59, −10).
Firm Size	Log of total assets for the most recent reporting period prior to the private placement. Reference is Annual Data Item Number 6 or Total Liabilities and Stockholder's Equity from page 5–21 of the User's Guide.

Table 2 Sample Characteristics of Equity Private Placements

The private placement sample includes 69 placements by 62 firms between 1/1/88 and 12/31/95. Each of the firms in the sample meet traditional requirements for available CRSP, *Compustat* and *Compaq Disclosure* data. Details on data development are available from the author on request. Eight of the firms are listed on one of the major exchanges with the remaining 61 trading on the Nasdaq or OTC Bulletin Board. Sixteen of the announcements affirm that the issues are of registered stock. Twenty-four are of unregistered stock. Twenty-nine of the announcements do not reveal the registration status of the privately placed stock. Proceeds are taken from the announcement. Fraction placed is expressed relative to total shares outstanding after the placement. The discount is measured relative to the share price five days before the announcement.

	Minimum	Mean	Median	Maximum
Proceeds (millions)	.175	4.890	2.200	22.500
Fraction Placed	.002	.122	.108	.395
Discount (Premium)	(.500)	.208	.207	.786

Issuing Activity	Year	Number Issues
	1988	4
	1989	4
	1990	3
	1991	4
	1992	7
	1993	13
	1994	16
	1995	18
Total Issues		69

Table 3 Sample Characteristics of Privately Placing Firms*

Descriptive data is given for the 69 privately placing firms. Firm
data are drawn from the most recently reported (prior to the
announcement date) *Compustat Full Coverage* and *Research Annual*
Files. Inside ownership and outstanding share data are taken from
the most recent available monthly data on *Compaq Disclosure.* Inside
Ownership is imputed for firms whose ownership data is not available until the period up to twelve months following the private
placement announcement. Market Value of Equity is the product of
outstanding shares times share price five days before the announcement. Total Assets is drawn from the annual *Compustat* files for the
year preceding the announcement. Book-to-Market Equity Ratio is
the ratio of stockholders equity from the prior year's *Compustat*
files divided by the market value of equity.

	Minimum	Mean	Median	Maximum
Firm Size (Total Assets, millions)	.499	17.497	10.608	71.921
Inside Ownership	.018	.256	.227	.826
Market Value of Equity (millions)	3.303	66.317	35.961	493.582
Book-to-Market Equity Ratio	−.001	.294	.177	1.65

*43 Firms in Financial Distress reporting 2 prior years negative earnings.

Table 4 Sample Characteristics of Purchasers of Private Equity Placements

Descriptive data are given for the purchasers of the 69 private placements of equity. All of the information provided below is taken from the announcement by the firm of their private equity placements. The announcements are drawn from the *Business News Wire* using combinations of the key words "private placement, private offering, private stock purchase, private purchase, private sale and private stake."

Purchaser Characteristic	Number of Purchasers
Single	9
Foreign	7
Institutional (Corporate)	24
Managers/Directors	9
Outsider Becoming Blockholder/Manager	11
Purchaser(s) Unknown	26

*The total number of purchasers sums to over 69 as many purchasers share multiple characteristics.

Table 5 Sample Characteristics of Proposed Uses of Private Equity Placement Proceeds

Descriptive data are given for the proposed uses by the issuing firms of their private equity placement proceeds. All of the information provided below is taken from the announcements.

Announced Funds Use	Number of Firms
New Product	34
Retire Debt	8
Working Capital	23
Acquisition	3
Use Unknown	14

*The total number of firms sums to over 69 as many firms report multiple intended uses for their equity private placement proceeds.

Table 6-A Selected Contrasts to Earlier Studies of Equity Private Placements

The 69 observations are contrasted to the data examined in earlier studies of private placements of equity. Contrasting data are drawn from Wruck (1989), Hertzel and Smith (1993) and Tables 2-5 of this study.

	Tables 2–5	Wruck	Hertzel & Smith
A. Purchaser Characteristics			
Managers/Directors	13%	13%	6%
Institutions	35%	27%	50%
Single/Individual	13%	11%	28%
B. Placement Characteristics			
Average Proceeds (millions)	4.89	31.46	38.98
Average Discount*	20.8%	4.8%	20.1%
Average Fraction Placed	12.2%	19.6%	16.5%
C. Firm Characteristics			
Average Market Value of Equity (millions)	66.32	233.7	441.5
Average Ownership Concentration pre-placement	25.6%	30.7%	30.3%

*A weighted estimate of the average discount to placement purchasers in the Wruck (1989) study is derived from the information provided in her study.

Table 6-B Selected Characteristics of the Private Placement Announcements Excluding Announcements by Sonic Environmental and Versus Technology

The 67 announcements in the final tests sample are contrasted to the 69 observations described in Tables 2–5.

	Tables 2–5	Final Tests Sample
A. Purchaser Characteristics		
Managers/Directors	13%	13%
Institutions	35%	34%
Single/Individual	13%	12%
B. Placement Characteristics		
Average Proceeds (millions)	4.89	5.01
Average Discount	20.8%	20.9%
Average Fraction Placed	12.2%	11.8%
Maximum Fraction Placed	39.5%	34.9%
Minimum Fraction Placed	.2%	.2%
Maximum Discount	78.6%	77.7%
Minimum Discount		
(Negative denotes premium)	–50.0%	–16.6%
C. Firm Characteristics		
Average Market Value of		
Equity (millions)	66.32	68.12
Average Ownership		
Concentration Pre-placement	25.6%	26%

Table 7 Cumulative Announcement Period Abnormal Returns

Sixty-nine private placement announcement period returns are examined. Cumulative abnormal returns (CAR) are calculated using the market model and the value-weighted index. Unadjusted returns are measured using Equation 9. Parameter estimates are calculated over the period (−200, −60). Adjusted returns are measured using Equation 10.

	Event Window					
	−59, 30	−29, −10	−9, 0	−3, 0	1, 10	−29, 10
A. *Unadjusted Returns*						
Mean CAR	−16.81	−18.43	.6123	.4871	−.001	−17.82
t-statistic	−14.72	−34.23	1.61	2.02	−.002	−23.40
P-values	.0001	.0001	.11	.04	.99	.0001
B. *Adjusted Returns*						
Mean CAR	28.64	−8.606	5.695	2.518	5.028	2.117
t-statistic	25.07	−15.99	14.96	10.46	13.21	2.780
P-values	.0001	.0001	.0001	.0001	.0001	.005

Table 8-A Predictions of an Optimal Liquidity Hypothesis

The dependent variable is the adjusted private placement cumulative abnormal return over the primary event window from 3 days before until the day of the announcement. A traditional market modeling with the estimation period (–200, –60) is employed. Factors from Equation 8 are proxied in Equation 11 by the selected independent variables.

Underlying factor from Equation 8	Selected proxy in Equation 11	Predicted Sign in Equation 11
A. *Growth options*	Earnings/price	–
	New product	+
	Working capital	+
B. *Ownership structure*	Single investor	+
	Foreign investor	+
	Management investor	+/–
	O'ship concentration level 1	+
	O'ship concentration level 2	–
	O'ship concentration level 3	+
	Retire debt	–/+
C. *Liquidity*	Liquidity	–
	Change in liquidity	+/–
D. *Control variables*	Financial distress	+/–
	Restricted shares	+
	Prior underperformance	+/–
	Firm size	–

Table 8-B Cross-Sectional Regression of Private Placement Announcement Period Abnormal Returns

The dependent variable is the adjusted private placement cumulative abnormal return over the primary event window from 3 days before until the day of the announcement. A traditional market modeling with the estimation period (–200, –60) is employed. Coefficients and p-values are calculated for 69 announcements from 1/1/88–12/31/95.

Independent Variable from Equation 11	Predicted Sign in Equation 11	Coefficient	P-Value
A. *Growth options*			
Earnings/price	–	–.776	.003
New product	+	.168	.167
Working capital	+	.229	.047
B. *Ownership structure*			
Single investor	+	.109	.628
Foreign investor	+	–.246	.243
Management investor	+/–	–.054	.752
O'ship concentration level 1	+	–.120	.569
O'ship concentration level 2	–	.068	.534
O'ship concentration level 3	+	–.052	.629
Retire debt	–/+	.162	.341
C. *Liquidity*			
Liquidity	–	–.093	.470
Change in liquidity	+	.138	.202
D. *Control variables*			
Financial distress	+/–	.000	.999
Restricted shares	+	–.124	.318
Prior under-performance	+/–	.122	.317
Firm size	–	–.101	.058
Intercept	n/a	.157	.492
White's Spec. Test	n/a	Chi-Square = 65.1	P-Value = .472
Adjusted R-squared value	n/a	Adj. R-sq. = .227	n/a

Table 8-C Cross-Sectional Regression of Private Placement Announcement Period Abnormal Returns without Allowance for Ownership Structure Changes

The dependent variable is the adjusted private placement cumulative abnormal return over the primary event window from 3 days before until the day of the announcement. A traditional market modeling with the estimation period (−200, −60) is employed. Coefficient estimates and p-values are calculated for the 69 announcements between January of 1988 and December of 1995, excluding proxies for ownership structure.

Independent Variable from Equation 11	Predicted Sign in Equation 11	Coefficient	P-Value
A. *Growth options*			
Earnings/price	−	−.733	.002
New product	+	.129	.220
Working capital	+	.216	.054
B. *Ownership structure*	n/a	n/a	n/a
C. *Liquidity*			
Liquidity	−	−.071	.561
Change in liquidity	+	.128	.181
D. *Control variables*			
Financial distress	+/−	−.007	.948
Restricted shares	+	−.113	.324
Prior under-performance	+/−	.084	.413
Firm size	−	−.108	.030
Intercept	n/a	.236	.271
White's Spec. Test	n/a	Chi-Square = 59	P-Value = .156
Adjusted R-squared value	n/a	Adj. R-sq. = .259	n/a

Table 8-D Cross-Sectional Regression of Private Placement Announcement Period Abnormal Returns without Allowance for Ownership Structure Changes or Firm Size and Excluding Two Highly Influential Observations

The dependent variable is the adjusted private placement cumulative abnormal return over the primary event window from 3 days before until the day of the announcement. A traditional market modeling with the estimation period (–200, –60) is employed. Coefficient estimates and p-values are calculated for 67 announcements between January of 1988 and December of 1995, excluding proxies for ownership structure and firm size.

Independent Variable from Equation 11	Predicted Sign in Equation 11	Coefficient	P-Value
A. *Growth options*			
Earnings/price	–	–.427	.013
New product	+	–.072	.306
Working capital	+	.008	.911
B. *Ownership structure*	n/a	n/a	n/a
C. *Liquidity*			
Liquidity	–	–.058	.437
Change in liquidity	+	.187	.001
D. *Control variables*			
Financial distress	+/–	–.009	.905
Restricted shares	+	.120	.112
Prior under- performance	+/–	–.114	.099
Firm size	n/a	n/a	n/a
Intercept	n/a	.041	.700
White's Spec. Test	n/a	Chi-Square = 51.6	P-Value = .086
Adjusted R-squared value	n/a	Adj. R-sq. = .276	n/a

Table 8-E Normative Cross-Sectional Regression of Private Placement Announcement Period Abnormal Returns

The dependent variable is the adjusted private placement cumulative abnormal return over the primary event window from 3 days before until the day of the announcement. A traditional market modeling with the estimation period (−200, −60) is employed. Coefficient estimates and p-values are calculated for the 67 announcements between January of 1988 and December of 1995, excluding proxies for ownership structure.

Independent Variable from Equation 11	Predicted Sign in Equation 11	Coefficient	P-Value
A. *Growth options*			
Earnings/price	−	−.451	.006
New product	+	−.085	.198
Working capital	+	−.017	.801
B. *Ownership structure*	n/a	n/a	n/a
C. *Liquidity*			
Liquidity	−	.003	.965
Change in liquidity	+	.122	.034
D. *Control variables*			
Financial distress	+/−	−.003	.962
Restricted shares	+	.103	.145
Prior under-performance	+/−	−.118	.068
Firm size	−	−.087	.004
Intercept	n/a	.277	.032
White's Spec. Test	n/a	Chi-Square = 62.6	P-Value = .092
Adjusted R-squared value	n/a	Adj. R-sq. = .367	n/a

Table 8-F Cross-Sectional Regression of Private Placement Announcement Period Abnormal Returns: Five-factor Iteration

The dependent variable is the adjusted private placement cumulative abnormal return over the primary event window from 3 days before until the day of the announcement. A traditional market modeling with the estimation period (−200, −60) is employed. Coefficient estimates and p-values are calculated for the 67 announcements between January of 1988 and December of 1995, excluding proxies for ownership structure and including the factors estimated below.

Independent Variable from Equation 11	Predicted Sign in Equation 11	Coefficient	P-Value
A. *Growth options*			
Earnings/price	−	−.441	.001
B. *Ownership structure*	n/a	n/a	n/a
C. *Liquidity*			
Liquidity	n/a	n/a	n/a
Change in liquidity	+	.115	.002
D. *Control variables*			
Restricted shares	+	.100	.128
Prior under-performance	+/−	.096	.092
Firm size	−	−.087	.002
Intercept	n/a	.226	.028
White's Spec. Test	n/a	Chi-Square = 32	P-Value = .022
Adjusted R-squared value	n/a	Adj. R-sq. = .389	n/a

Table 8-G Cross-Sectional Regression of Private Placement Announcement Period Abnormal Returns: Four-factor Iteration

The dependent variable is the adjusted private placement cumulative abnormal return over the primary event window from 3 days before until the day of the announcement. A traditional market modeling with the estimation period (−200, −60) is employed. Coefficient estimates and p-values are calculated for the 67 announcements between January of 1988 and December of 1995, excluding proxies for ownership structure and including the factors estimated below.

Independent Variable from Equation 11	Predicted Sign in Equation 11	Coefficient	P-Value
A. *Growth options*			
Earnings/price	−	−.418	.003
B. *Ownership structure*	n/a	n/a	n/a
C. *Liquidity*			
Liquidity	−	−.047	.483
Change in liquidity	+	.141	.008
D. *Control variables*			
Firm size	−	−.089	.003
Intercept	n/a	.280	.001
White's Spec. Test	n/a	Chi-Square = 26.9	P-Value = .020
Adjusted R-squared value	n/a	Adj. R-sq. = .360	n/a

Table 8-H Cross-Sectional Regression of Private Placement Announcement Period Abnormal Returns: Three-factor Iteration

The dependent variable is the adjusted private placement cumulative abnormal return over the primary event window from 3 days before until the day of the announcement. A traditional market modeling with the estimation period (–200, –60) is employed. Coefficient estimates and p-values are calculated for the 67 announcements between January of 1988 and December of 1995, excluding proxies for ownership structure and including the factors estimated below.

Independent Variable Equation 11	Predicted Sign in Equation 11	Coefficient	P-Value
A. *Growth options*			
Earnings/price	–	–.426	.002
B. *Ownership structure*	n/a	n/a	n/a
C. *Liquidity*			
Liquidity	n/a	n/a	n/a
Change in liquidity	+	.115	.002
D. *Control variables*			
Firm size	–	–.096	.001
Intercept	n/a	.283	.001
White's Spec. Test	n/a	Chi-Square = 22.4	P-Value = .008
Adjusted R-squared value	n/a	Adj. R-sq. = .365	n/a

Table 8-I Cross-Sectional Regression of Private Placement Announcement Period Abnormal Returns with an Allowance for Changes in Ownership Concentration

The dependent variable is the adjusted private placement cumulative abnormal return over the primary event window from 3 days before until the day of the announcement. A traditional market modeling with the estimation period (−200, −60) is employed. Coefficient estimates and p-values are calculated for the 67 announcements between January of 1988 and December of 1995. Changes in levels of inside ownership concentration for levels from 0–5, 5–25 and over 25% are calculated for each firm as a result of the private placements.

Independent Variable from Equation 11	Predicted Sign in Equation 11	Coefficient	P-Value
A. *Growth options*			
Earnings/price	−	−.294	.111
New product	+	−.144	.026
Working capital	+	−.082	.241
B. *Ownership structure*			
Change in Level 1	+	15.659	.168
Change in Level 2	−	−1.948	.093
Change in Level 3	+	.663	.119
C. *Liquidity*			
Liquidity	−	−.062	.343
Change in liquidity	+	.193	.002
D. *Control variables*			
Financial distress	+/−	−.006	.934
Restricted shares	+	.067	.391
Prior under-performance	+/−	−.153	.020
Firm size	−	−.090	.002
Intercept	n/a	.378	.008
White's Spec. Test	n/a	Chi-Square = 60.56	P-Value = .492
Adjusted R-squared value	n/a	Adj. R-sq. = .474	n/a

Table 9 Cumulative Announcement Period Abnormal Returns Excluding Announcements by Sonic Environmental and Versus Technology

Cumulative abnormal returns (CAR) are calculated using the market model and the value-weighted index. Unadjusted returns are calculated using Equation 9. Parameter estimates are calculated over the period (–200, –60). A traditional market modeling is employed. Sixty-seven announcements are examined between January of 1988 and December of 1995. Adjusted returns are calculated using Equation 10.

	Event Window	
	(-59, 30)	(-3, 0)
A. *Unadjusted Returns*		
Mean CAR	-17.35	.378
t-statistic	-15.19	1.57
P-values	.001	.117
B. *Adjusted Returns*		
Mean CAR	25.68	2.28
t-statistic	22.16	9.31
P-values	.001	.001

Table 10-A VIF's for a Cross-Sectional Modeling of Adjusted Abnormal Returns

Variance inflation factor ranges are provided for the models of Tables 8B through 8H.

Independent Variable	Variance Inflation Factor Range
A. *Growth options*	
Earnings/price	1.008–1.687
New product	1.287–1.636
Working capital	1.303–1.387
B. *Ownership structure*	
Single investor	1.548
Foreign investor	1.337
Management investor	1.485
O'ship concentration level 1	1.597
O'ship concentration level 2	1.328
O'ship concentration level 3	1.251
Retire debt	
C. *Liquidity*	
Liquidity	2.093–2.638
Change in liquidity	1.081–3.304
D. *Control variables*	
Financial distress	1.594–1.804
Restricted shares	1.088–1.343
Prior underperformance	1.070–1.668
Firm size	1.085–1.400

Table 10-B Pearson Correlation Coefficients for the Variables Describing Private Placement Adjusted Abnormal Returns

Pearson correlation coefficients are provided for the OLS modeling of Equation 11. Independent variables are drawn from the model of Table 8-E. P-values are in parentheses.

VAR	E/P	NP	WC	LQ0	CHG	FD	URG	UND	SIZE
E/P	1.00	-.023 (.852)	.102 (.410)	.043 (.728)	.002 (.982)	-.456 (.001)	-.023 (.848)	-.103 (.407)	-.060 (.629)
NP		1.00	-.397 (.001)	.183 (.138)	.213 (.084)	.018 (.884)	-.043 (.730)	-.227 (.065)	-.054 (.663)
WC			1.00	-.198 (.108)	-.083 (.507)	.017 (.890)	.060 (.627)	-.209 (.090)	-.138 (.266)
LQ0				1.00	.676 (.001)	.114 (.358)	-.337 (.005)	-.155 (.209)	-.274 (.025)
CHG					1.00	.332 (.006)	-.113 (.364)	-.155 (.209)	-.274 (.024)
FD						1.00	-.059 (.633)	-.178 (.149)	-.081 (.517)
URG							1.00	.180 (.145)	-.157 (.203)
UND								1.00	.081 (.516)
SIZE									1.00

E/P represents Earnings/Price, NP stands for New Product, WC is Working Capital, LQ0 is Initial Liquidity, CHG is the abbreviation for the Change in Liquidity, FD stands for Financial Distress, URG represents Unregistered or Restricted Securities, UND is for Prior Underperformance and SIZE represents Firm Size.

Table 11-A White Standard Errors and Heteroskedastic Corrected T-values

White's method is used to correct t-statistics for heteroskedasticity in the modeling of Table 8-E. Parameter estimates are divided by the square root of the relevant diagonal element of the "consistent covariance of estimates matrix" to provide a heteroskedasticity-corrected t-value.

Independent Variable	Uncorrected t-value	Corrected t-value
A. *Growth options*		
Earnings/price	−2.882	−2.465
New product	−1.302	−1.513
Working capital	−.253	−.300
B. *Ownership structure*	n/a	n/a
C. *Liquidity*		
Liquidity	.043	.051
Change in liquidity	2.172	2.139
D. *Control variables*		
Financial distress	−.047	−.065
Restricted shares	1.477	1.673
Prior underperformance	−1.856	−2.092
Firm size	−3.050	−4.870

Table 11-B White Standard Errors and Heteroskedastic Corrected T-values

White's method is used to correct t-statistics for heteroskedasticity in the modeling of Table 8-F. Parameter estimates are divided by the square root of the relevant diagonal element of the "consistent covariance of estimates matrix" to provide a heteroskedasticity-corrected t-value.

Independent Variable	Uncorrected t-value	Corrected t-value
A. *Growth options*		
Earnings/price	−3.348	−2.833
B. *Ownership structure*	n/a	n/a
C. *Liquidity*		
Liquidity	n/a	n/a
Change in liquidity	3.222	2.697
D. *Control variables*		
Restricted shares	1.544	1.828
Prior underperformance	−1.715	−1.886
Firm size	−3.235	−2.723

Table 12-A Post-Event Parameter Estimation for the Full Sample of 69 Announcements of Private Placements of Equity

Cumulative abnormal returns (CAR) are calculated using the market model with the value-weighted index. The pre-event estimation period is (−200, −60). The post-event estimation period is (11,151). Unadjusted returns using post-event parameter estimates are provided in Panel A. Adjusted returns using the post-event parameter estimates are given in Panel B. Event windows are encouraged by Wruck (1989) and Hertzel and Smith (1993).

	Event Window					
	−59, 30	−29, −10	−9, 0	−3, 0	1, 10	−29, 10
A. *Unadjusted Returns*						
Mean CAR	-15.08	-17.15	.8468	.3557	.1655	-16.14
t-statistic	-13.20	-31.85	2.224	1.477	.4349	-21.19
P-values	.0001	.0001	.0261	.1369	.6636	.0001
B. *Adjusted Returns*						
Mean CAR	25.94	-8.308	5.441	2.189	4.715	1.848
t-statistic	22.71	-15.43	14.29	9.09	12.39	2.427
P-values	.0001	.0001	.0001	.0001	.0001	.015

Table 12-B Post-Event Parameter Estimation for the Sample Excluding Highly Influential Announcements by Sonic Environmental and Versus Technology

Cumulative abnormal returns (CAR) are calculated using the market model with the value-weighted index. The pre-event estimation period is (–200, –60). The post-event estimation period is (11,151). Unadjusted returns using post-event parameter estimates are provided in Panel A. Adjusted returns using the post-event parameter estimates are given in Panel B. Event windows are encouraged by Wruck (1989) and Hertzel and Smith (1993).

	Event Window					
	–59, 30	–29, –10	–9, 0	–3, 0	1, 10	–29, 10
A. *Unadjusted Returns*						
Mean CAR	–15.50	–17.70	.9071	.3002	.1505	–16.64
t-statistic	–13.57	–32.88	2.383	1.247	.3953	–21.86
P-values	.0001	.0001	.0171	.2125	.6926	.0001
B. Adjusted Returns						
Mean CAR	27.79	–8.049	5.682	2.210	4.926	2.560
t-statistic	23.98	–14.73	14.71	9.046	12.75	3.313
P-values	.0001	.0001	.0001	.0001	.0001	.0009

Figure 1 Optimal Liquidity Level for the Firm

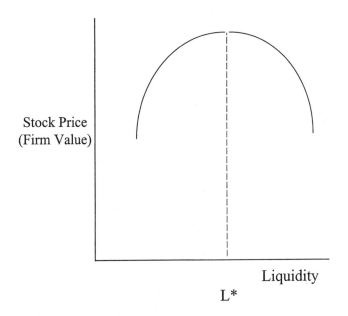

Stock Price
(Firm Value)

Liquidity

L*

* Global minimum cost of liquidity.

Figure 2 Optimal Liquidity Level for the Growing Firm

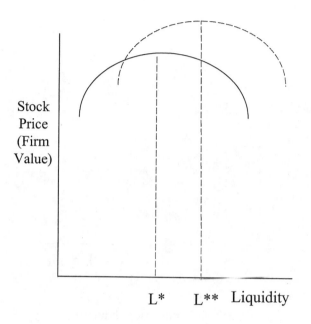

Stock
Price
(Firm
Value)

L*   L**   Liquidity

** Minimum cost of liquidity for the growing firm.

Figure 2a Changing Liquidity Optima for the Growing Firm

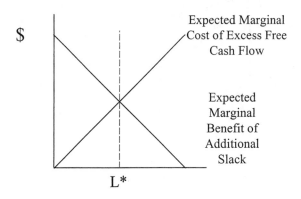

Figure 2b Benefits/Optima Shift

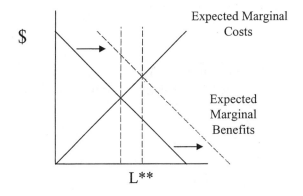

** Minimum cost of liquidity for the growing firm.

Figure 3 Optimal Liquidity Level with an Entrenched Management

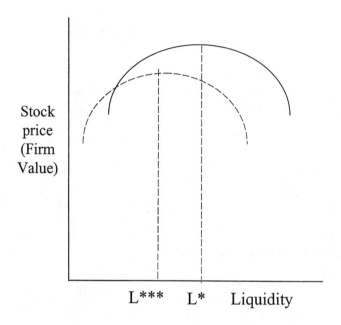

*** Minimum cost of liquidity for the firm with an
entrenched management.

Figure 3a Changing Liquidity Optimum with an Entrenched Management

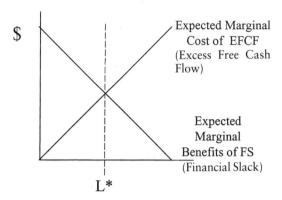

$ | Expected Marginal
Cost of EFCF
(Excess Free Cash
Flow)

Expected
Marginal
Benefits of FS
(Financial Slack)

L*

Figure 3b Costs/Optima Shift

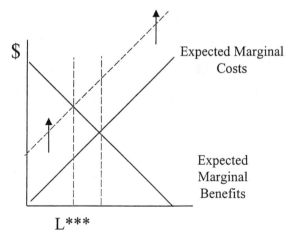

$ | Expected Marginal
Costs

Expected
Marginal
Benefits

L***

*** Minimum cost of liquidity for the firm with an
entrenched management.

Figure 4 Neutral Stock Price Response for an Excess Flow of Liquidity to a Slack-Poor Firm

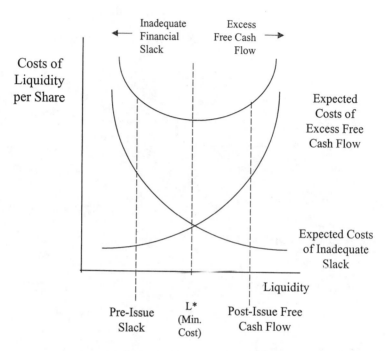

* Global minimum cost of liquidity.

Author Index

Subject Index